Will the Real Human Being Please Stand Up!

Discovering Your Hidden Self

by
Jean Marie Van Derhoff
Psychological Clairvoyant

Will the Real Human Being Please Stand Up!

Discovering Your Hidden Self

by
Jean Marie Van Derhoff
Psychological Clairvoyant

Kravitz & Sons
INNOVATORS IN PUBLISHING, MARKETING AND ADVERTISING

Kravitz and Sons LLC
204 E Arlington Blvd. Suite B
Greenville, NC 27858

Published by Kravitz and Sons LLC.

ISBN: 979-8-89639-420-4 (sc)
ISBN: 979-8-89639-419-8 (e)
ISBN: 979-8-89639-436-5 (hc)

Library of Congress Control Number: 2025919615

Contents

Preface

In this book, I clairvoyantly recount in detail a person's physical, mental, and emotional life from conception through birth. Month by month I describe factual aspects of an unborn baby's growth processes: physical as well as psychological.

I share in detail my clairvoyant studies of the intentions, thoughts, feelings, and psychic actions of parents in relation to their unborn child. I show how an unborn baby's choices in reaction to parents are the foundation for his or her life experiences and include medical, scientific facts that confirm my clairvoyant observations.

The book pertains not only to unborn babies and infants. It also significantly reflects the psychological development of all humans. This original work is overflowing with new perspectives, insights, and lots of advice on how to become a better person.

You will discover answers to questions about yourself. New understanding will inspire and challenge you in your everyday life. You will become aware of how you have created many of your behaviors and how to change what you don't like. You will see the importance of making every day and every choice count. You will know how to act instead of reacting. You will recognize how to mentally and emotionally interact with your unborn baby or infant. You will have the tools to make your life truly more meaningful.

Lastly, by reading the excerpts and working with the perspectives in this book, you will be aspiring to become a person who excels not only in life but also in love. Your focus and your goal will be on becoming a more genuine and loving Human Being.

Introduction

I'd like to begin this journey with our commonality, that is, our basic human makeup, and explain many misunderstood or even unknown (by some) aspects of a Human Being.

All of us were conceived and lived for nine months in our mothers' wombs. By the time of birth, we have already become distinctive personalities. Most of the source of our actions and reactions that is, our behavior, can be traced right back into the womb. Our most important and most basic choices were made when we were only fetuses. All our choices, while in the womb and up until now, are still within us; they are recorded in our subconscious.

We all have had diverse experiences and have made different choices either in relation to, or in reaction to, our individual circumstances. It is our choices that have created our uniquely different characters and personalities. I will demonstrate this by recounting excerpts from my clairvoyant readings of psychic and subconscious interactions between parents and babies, which describe the effects of specific choices.

Human Beings are pure potential! We are not innately good, and we are not innately bad. Our choices determine our positive or negative attitudes and behaviors. A baby's choices, either in response to or, in reaction to parents have formed his or her behavior. I suspect you will relate to many of the choices and reactions narrated in this book. Even though we are unique, we are not all that dissimilar in how we respond and react.

Scientific evidence has confirmed most of my clairvoyant work. It has proven that a baby has already developed an individual personality by the time of birth. I will discuss why and how we choose varied intentions, have different attitudes, and form unique personalities.

An unborn baby displays many varied responses in relation to his or her mother, father, and the environment. These choices can be dramatically different—positive or negative—creating a positive or negative experience within the baby and the womb environment.

Our behavior develops because of our choices. Choices to react that are repeated over and over in the womb become behavioral patterns that we continue to develop after we are born. These behaviors stay with us and become subconscious driving forces that we often believe we have no control over. We view them as genetic or having another cause that is in line with our individual beliefs.

The choices we have made while in the womb have substantially shaped our characters and personalities usually for a lifetime. We must get to the core truth about who we are, how we are made, and why we do what we do if we are ever to become truly content and satisfied Human Beings.

When we understand the source of our choices we will have the power to consciously change our intentions, thoughts, feelings and actions at will. Our psychological selves will no longer be a mystery to us. We will stop wanting to blame how we are, think, and feel on outside circumstances or other people. Claiming this responsibility gives us the power to change what we want to change within ourselves.

One
The Basics

"Awareness and free choice are essential, innate human abilities that we use for good or bad every second of our lives."

Let's get clear on how we have been created and who we are essentially as Human Beings. We have been created with two very important abilities: the ability to be aware and the ability to choose freely. Our awareness and free choice are in relation to the dynamic living realities of love, truth, rightness, and loving responsibility.

I say loving responsibility because there are two kinds of responsibility—loving responsibility and selfish responsibility. You can see the results of selfish responsibility all around us in the creations of people who greatly control to accomplish selfish goals. Their actions may seem positive and responsible at times, but to the degree that their actions are selfish they are hurtful.

We possess the ability to recognize, know, and choose for the living realities of love, truth, rightness, and loving responsibility. In fact, we do choose for or against love, truth, rightness, and loving responsibility at every moment and in every situation in our lives. The most essential aspect of a Human Being's behavior is his or her intention. Your intention is the core of every choice you make. Your intention determines the quality of your inner and outer life.

Who are we? What is the whole package? We are beings who create intentions and possess a will, a mind, an energetic body, a physical body, an ability to feel, and an ability to act. When we confuse these facts, we are confused about our very nature.

You are not your intentions; you have intentions. You are not your will; you have a will. You are not your mind; you have a mind. You are not your feelings; you have feelings. You are not your energetic body; you have an energetic body. You are not your physical body; you have a physical body—that includes your brain. You are not your brain; you have a brain (contrary to some current professional psychological belief).

What about these elements of ourselves? How do we get to really understand them? I would say firstly, not by listening to professionals. They have been steering us in the wrong *"It's not your fault"* direction for a long time. In all honesty, psychological professionals are saying that your behavior and problems are not your fault; that means they are not your responsibility.

There are many shades of gray in what they have come to believe and tell us about ourselves. The truth is always clear. It is never gray. *"When you discover the truth, it will be simple."* That also goes for the truth about yourself. We complicate our psyches as a way of trying to avoid the truth about ourselves. Who else can possibly be responsible for your choices—intentions, thoughts, feelings, and actions? Is there someone in there beside you? Oh, could it be your genes or your brain? What professionals propose does not even make sense.

We always have awareness and free choice. These two abilities make us fully responsible for everything we intend, think, feel, and do, period. The responsibility for our life's choices is real. We experience the effects of our choices whether we acknowledge that responsibility or not. We cannot change what is real and true. That means that we feel the positive or negative effects of our choices on an immediate, day-to-day basis whether we acknowledge that we are responsible or not.

We have complicated our psyches to such a degree that it takes much introspection and evaluation to even begin to unravel the layers we have built within our consciousnesses.

Let's talk about focusing on and living with your intentions, choices, thoughts, feelings, and actions. Selfreflection and introspection are primary. Study your intentions, thoughts, feelings, and actions as you would any subject you were passionate about learning.

Examine your intentions. This is core. This is where you can start in a certain (perhaps negative) situation, or outcome of a choice. A good way to track back to your true intention is to study your reasons or excuses for doing, or not doing, a specific thing. Excuses often point to a wrong intention. This is not always the case, but typically, why do we need to make an excuse for a right intention or motive? Honesty with self can be difficult, but it is completely necessary.

Intention is rarely talked about. I think most of us sidestep the reality of our true intentions because they show the underlying truth about us. In some way or another, most of our intentions are typically selfish. Most of us don't want to acknowledge this, even to ourselves. We may be *"hard-wired"* to be selfish, but we always possess the ability to choose to go against our selfish inclinations.

Understanding your will is of the utmost importance. The human will is vastly misunderstood. The human will has only two stances—*willing* or *willful.* You use the power of your choice to choose to be willing or willful in any given moment or situation. When the term willpower is used it is a fighting stance, which makes it a willful stance. There is no need for willpower when you are truly willing to do something that you know is right or willing not to do something that you know is wrong. You can surely feel the energetic difference between when you are willing and when you are willful.

Your choice is an expression of your will. We have created patterns of behavior by consistently choosing various intentions, thoughts, feelings, and actions. Yes! You choose every intention before you intend it. You choose every thought before you think it. You choose every feeling before you feel it. You choose every action before you take it. Do these ideas seem odd to you? If you observe yourself closely, you can see yourself choosing at every single moment.

You change your intentions at will. You do it all the time. This may be difficult to see at first because we are not always honest about our intentions.

You change your thoughts at will. You do it all the time. You can watch yourself going from one thought to another. You can see this especially when you want to focus on a precise topic, and your mind wanders. You choose to bring it back to what you wanted to focus on. But even saying *"your mind wanders"* as if it was doing it all by itself is not accurate! We are choosing every step of the way. If we ever get this one, our lives will be so much easier!

You change your feelings at will. You do it all the time. This is another instance where it may at first be difficult to realize. This is because we often allow ourselves to be driven by our subconscious choices to want something or to react in fear or anger to a person or situation.

You change your actions at will. You do it all the time. We can observe ourselves changing our behavior although it often seems difficult. It sometimes seems impossible. It is as if we were created a certain way and we just can't change, at least not certain things. Again, this pertains to our subconscious drives—that is, a subconscious choice to enact certain behavior patterns and react in seemingly automatic ways. The subconscious choice is more essential, so it wins out unless we work to change it.

We need to remember that we are Human Beings who are constantly using our wills. We are constantly choosing! There is never a moment when we are not choosing. Not one thing about us, not one thing about the whole of us is automatic, random, or outside of our conscious or subconscious direction and control.

It is important to consciously know that we actually ARE choosing and to consciously know HOW we are choosing. This is the beginning of taking personal responsibility for our behavior no matter what that behavior may be. It is the beginning of building a character that is truly solid in the living realities of love, truth, rightness, and loving responsibility. To the extent that we accomplish this, we will be viewed as a person of integrity with a caring attitude for those around us. And yet, there must be millions of people who genuinely love and are never noticed. Many times, they are even judged and their actions are misunderstood! When we have a selfish perspective, it is easy to view right as wrong and wrong as right! We like to judge others when we subconsciously see that they are making truly right choices, and we know that we are not.

Our physical makeup, and to some extent, our physical attributes come from the genes we have inherited. But, make no mistake, how you choose to intend, think, feel, and act, (that is, your behavior) comes directly from your spirit, your soul, if you will. It comes from who you are—a Human Being who has the ultimate choice to determine HOW you will be in any given moment or situation.

There may be times that you feel you don't have control over your intentions, thoughts, feelings, and actions. This is never true. You always possess the ability to choose for what is right, loving, honest, and lovingly responsible. However, you (and all of us) turn away from that ability and allow yourself to be driven by the destructive patterns and desires that you have buried in your subconscious. At these precise times, you have consciously made the decision to enact your deeper, truer destructive intentions and desires.

When you allow your subconscious drives to take over is when you feel you need to have willpower. You think that you need *"willpower"* when you are trying to consciously force yourself to go against your subconscious intentions, patterns, and desires. We believe we need *"willpower"* when we try to avoid the responsibility that we have for our true intentions, choices, thoughts, feelings, and actions.

We become like two hand puppets fighting each other. The *"good"* puppet may win out for a minute or two, but the *"bad"* puppet is enacting your true, most basic intention to do whatever it is that you are *"trying"* not to do. The *"bad"* puppet always wins in the end unless you change your true intention. We have all had this experience from the smallest temptation to the most severe.

"Willpower" is not the answer. We need to go deeper! The good news is that we do have the power to go deeper. We do have the power to change our subconscious intention (and in doing so, change our thoughts, feelings, and actions). But (and this is a huge but) to do this we need to be sincerely willing. We need to be willing to do what we know is right sincerely, for no other reason than it is the right thing to do. This applies to all situations. Sincere willingness (not willpower) to do the right thing in a situation is the answer to defusing our strongest desires, patterns, and drives!

Understanding the conscious part of your mind: If you are confusing your mind with your brain, it is really this simple. Your brain is a component of your physical body. Your mind is an expression of your being, that is, your essence, your substance, the part of you who lives on after your physical body has gone to ashes.

You use your brain to process your choices—intentions, thoughts, feelings, and actions. Your brain is your tool, and nothing more. Your brain cannot make you do something. You, the being, the Human Being, choose, intend, and act. When we don't have these simple facts, our lives are chaotic, and we become like small boats on an ocean without rudders.

It is true that our brains can wear out like the rest of us. However, this is tricky. Just as we can live a physically healthy life by doing the right things to take care of our bodies (something most of us don't do) in the same manner, how we intend and choose in relation to love, truth, rightness, and loving responsibility has an enormous effect on our mental and emotional condition late in life, as well as every step along the way.

Most of our physical and mental ailments have been created by our individual choices. I don't know why we don't really get this fact. I can choose to be healthy into old age by learning how to treat my body (including my brain) to achieve that purpose. With the Internet at our disposal, this is not a difficult task. There are exceptions but, for most of us, we can trace any physical disease back to poor eating habits, inordinate stress, and other mental, emotional, and physical choices that we felt driven to make, but did not have to make. Also, and importantly, when we are sincerely willing we can also trace any mental and emotional *"disease"* back to our choices starting in the womb.

When we experience negative physical conditions in our bodies (including our brains) it is safe to assume that we are, in some way, responsible. This is when it becomes past time that we examined our intentions and choices to see how we have come to the physical state and/or mental state in which we find ourselves.

When you ask yourself enough questions, you will eventually begin to ask yourself the right questions in order to come to a beginning point to heal. To know and believe that your choices brought you to the condition in which you find yourself will give you the power to change that condition or change yourself accordingly.

There are exceptions to what I am saying but, for most of us, what I am saying is true. Taking a position of true and loving responsibility for our choices can only lead to true healing in one area or another. Physical choices may have propelled us over the guard rail, and as we are sailing through the air, the only right choice might be to accept the inevitable outcome with loving responsibility. This is not the end for us, and a loving, accepting attitude would certainly carry us to a better place!

You don't need a psychotherapist or a regression therapist to help you understand your subconscious. Certainly, you don't need a therapist to understand your conscious self. With enough willingness and honesty, you can do it yourself! Truly, with the way most therapists think these days, you are better off doing it yourself.

If you believe that your condition (whatever it may be) is not of your creation and it is not your fault, you probably believe that it is not your responsibility. How can you change a behavior or a drive that you tell yourself is outside of your control? How can you change a behavior that you tell yourself you have not intentionally created? I'm sure there are well-meaning therapists out there; however, if a person is coming from a place that is one step away from the truth, you may as well be a thousand steps away because you'll never get the right answer!

There seems to be 12-step cures for everything, yet we are all still struggling with our individual "addictions." This is because within the 12-step programs they tell you, and you believe, that you are helpless to change without God. You can't do it yourself. You need God.

This is a _twist_ on the truth, so that makes it at least one step away from the truth. When you believe that forces, other than your own intention and choice, are causing your negative mental and emotional condition and that you need an outside source to help you heal, there is absolutely no hope for true, positive change.

Those *"demons"* will always be lurking to reclaim your intentions, thoughts, feelings, and actions. This is the reason *"they say"* an alcoholic will always be an alcoholic and cannot take one drink without regressing. Regression comes because you have not changed the source of the problem, which is your subconscious intention and choice to enact specific subconscious behavior patterns and drives.

Here's the <u>twist</u> on the truth about needing God's help. When you were conceived in your mother's womb, God gave you all the tools you needed. He did not make you *"flawed."* Besides, you really cannot *"inherit"* (psychologically) someone else's choice, or the effects of a choice.

At every moment of your existence you experience your ability to choose freely. Your psychological attributes and experience are the result of your choices. It was your negative and reactive choices that you began making while in the womb, which created patterns within you, that made you appear to be flawed, helpless, and selfishly driven.

Just one step away from the truth, you might as well be a thousand steps away because you'll never get the right answer! Again, God gave us awareness and free choice at the very beginning. You always had the power to choose rightly. You always had the awareness to know the right choice and the ability to do it. Can any of us deny this fact? You may say that you knew the right choice but did not have the strength to act on it. Your drives took over, and you could not help yourself. That is why you needed God to intervene. After much effort and praying on your part, He saved you from your demons. One truth, that we just don't want to get, is that we always have the ability to make the right choice. We all know that our wrong choices cause us and others pain, and we have no genuine excuse for them.

Have I gotten off the track? What does all this have to do with the subconscious? My answer is everything! We have created our demons by choices to subconsciously trigger and enact destructive, self-destructive, and self-serving reactive drives.

Our demons are a manifestation of our wrong subconscious intentions, thoughts, feelings, and actions. Our conscious choice to activate them is the trigger. Our hand on the dial determines the intensity. We alone have the power to activate our demons or to defuse them. This is what our free will is all about. We have free choice and the ability to act rightly at every moment, no matter how driven we feel ourselves to be, or how flawed and hopeless we believe that we are.

Demons—this word has got me thinking. I don't think of drives as demons. To me they are subconscious choices to be willful and enact behavior patterns and programs that we have built in our subconscious memories, starting in the womb. When I share excerpts from my clairvoyant readings of the subconscious of people displaying various dysfunctions (and, also just ordinary folk) how this works will become apparent.

What about the subconscious in general? What is it? How does it work? The most important fact to know about your subconscious is that this is where you, the being, the Human Being, live on your most essential level. You, the being, control all the elements of your subconscious and conscious mind. You control all the complicated functions of your physical body and most likely other aspects that I don't know about.

At each moment, you determine the quality and outcome of your inner and outer life by your conscious and subconscious intentions and choices, from the smallest everyday choices to the biggest fork in the road life decisions. Every choice we make is significant and has positive or negative effects and consequences.

It is so hard for us to get this! But, you will never fully understand it, or even believe it, unless you are willing to take the full responsibility that is yours, for your every intention and choice. Blame is your biggest enemy when you are attempting to understand and access your subconscious mind. It robs you of the truth, the truth about who you are on the essential level of your being.

You the Being—Your Subconscious (Psychic) Life

The most fascinating facts about your subconscious are who you are; and what you do on that energetic psychic level. You have an entire subconscious life the way you have a conscious life. You are only subtly aware of it at times; and sometimes not conscious of it at all.

What is even more amazing is that Human Beings function on two levels of consciousness at the exact same time. At any given moment, you have a subconscious in tention and a conscious intention! You have a subconscious thought and a conscious thought! You have a subconscious feeling and a conscious feeling! You enact a subconscious action and a conscious action all simultaneously!

Intentions, thoughts, and feelings are not physical. It is understandable that we can create and regulate them within our subconscious minds. But, what about our actions? Don't we need a physical body to act? No, we do not. We act in our energetic bodies on a psychic realm. We do this by sending people thoughts, feelings, and sometimes the hurtful energies of anger or the like. When an angry energy is strong it can cause physical pain in the body of the person we are angry with and psychically attacking.

Most of us are not even aware of having an energetic body, much less living our lives through it. I think the biggest reason we don't want to acknowledge the subconscious part of ourselves is that we can be extremely selfish. Negative intentions, thoughts, feelings, and actions on a subconscious level cannot be rationalized as positive because on that essential level they are seen in truth.

However, the very same negative intentions, thoughts, feelings, and actions can be consciously ration alized as being right and positive. We can manipulate the truth (only in our minds!) with our "*good reasons*" and excuses. We use them to cover and cloud the truth of what we are really intending and doing. In my opinion, not being willing to be aware of our subconscious selves is a huge problem. The reason why we are not aware of our subconscious is that we want to continue to make excuses for our wrong intentions, thoughts, feelings, and actions. More than that, we want to keep making wrong choices and keep making our wrongness "*right.*"

Most of us ordinary folk do a fair amount of controlling, or at least influencing, the people in our lives by psychically projecting our desires, wishes, demands and the like onto them. We may even make psychic threats or attack with energy to accomplish our goals. This is most harmful when done with our unborn babies, newborns, and infants. They are particularly impressionable and are in a physically helpless position; which makes them enormously susceptible to our wishes and demands. It also makes them fearful of our energetic attacks and even the potential of an attack.

Of course, we also send love energy and good thoughts and feelings. But this can be extremely tricky when we don't know exactly what we are doing on a psychic level. Besides, we may not consciously know our true subconscious intention. Even when praying for someone we can be energetically imposing our demands on the person, or even bombarding him or her with energy that we tell ourselves is loving or good for them. The truth is that we make most of our destructive and hurtful choices subconsciously. This is our biggest problem.

This entire concept (reality) is so far from what we think of as real; for clarity, I would like to explain it another way. We become split by choosing to have two opposite intentions, thoughts, feelings, and actions. We do this to pretend that we are not at cause in the disasters and problems within us and in our lives.

We can be holding a destructive or self-destructive intention while, at the same time, telling ourselves that our intention, or motive, is good or gives us some benefit. Most of us do this often and it is to our great detriment. We strike out subconsciously at those close to us, including our children while only barely sensing that we are doing wrong. When we get angry or become Mr. or Mrs. Nasty, that is only the tip of the subconscious iceberg! We make many justifications for our negative behavior just so we can believe that we are good or doing the right thing in that moment.

So often we see right as wrong and wrong as right. Or, we sometimes even deny that there is a right and a wrong in all situations. No wonder we are so complicated and so purposefully confused about our inner life and our behavior.

If we would only face the truth about our true intentions at those times we could heal ourselves. In addition, we could instigate healing in those close, especially our children. But no! We don't want to admit that we are wrong (especially to our children) so we continue with our emotional pain and justify our hurtful intentions, thoughts, feelings, and actions. I can say these things because I've seen this again and again, sometimes to my disbelief! I knew two severely abusive parents who refused to admit their abuse of their son to a judge to try to lessen his heavy sentence. They did not want to appear wrong, even though they were totally wrong. This sounds extreme but it is not as uncommon as you might imagine.

When your conscious intention is the same as your good and right subconscious intention you are not splitting yourself. You are being honest. You feel a sense of wholeness. Truly right choices make you feel good and give you a sense of wholeness and content. In that moment, you are not splitting yourself by having a false positive conscious intention superimposed over a deeper selfish subconscious intention.

Nonetheless, when a person has a destructive subconscious intention and is enacting it with full conscious knowledge and awareness, there is no honesty here. There is only severe complication and hurtful craziness because such a person is *"jumping ship"* on who he or she was meant to be: a loving Human Being.

Our primary purpose in life is to love the life around us. The current idea that you must be able to love yourself before you can love anyone else, has been totally misconstrued for selfish convenience. Actually, it is the exact opposite. When you are willing to have your attention off yourself and out in a truly loving, caring way, you are expressing love; and in that way, you are loving yourself!

There is never a valid excuse for not loving the life around us. When we act against this primary purpose we always feel the negative effects, as does all the life around us! You never need to wonder what your purpose in life is; when you truly love you will realize that your purpose is to love. You've got it; you can then branch out from that place.

The sad fact is that, for most of us, having a matching truly right conscious and subconscious intention is somewhat of a rare occurrence. Our deepest intention is often selfish, that is, ultimately wanting something for self. We know this is somehow wrong to one extent or another, so we tell ourselves that our intention for a certain action is different than it is in reality. Again, honest introspection is crucial to self-awareness and awareness in general.

Here is a not-so-serious example of your subconscious intention being different from your conscious intention. After hurting someone's feelings, you may catch yourself saying, *"Oh, I didn't mean that!"* But, guess what? Yes, you did. It was coming straight out of your subconscious intention which was in some way self-serving and hurtful. Our subconscious intentions, thoughts, feelings, and actions are often negative. There is no need to hide our loving intentions, thoughts, feelings, and actions because we all know that that is the way we are supposed to be! We greatly confuse ourselves (on purpose) when our conscious intentions, thoughts, feelings, and actions are different from our subconscious ones.

Babies in the womb, infants and young children respond to our subconscious lives, especially when our intentions are concerning them. They do not know language yet and communicate by reading our subconscious intentions, thoughts, feelings, and actions, the same as (or better than) a clairvoyant such as I might do. They also communicate their reactions and responses to parents by sending thoughts in the form of feelings and pictures. This is truly amazing to experience. It is worth the effort of becoming more inwardly honest and clear to be able to see this, especially if you are a parent. But again, to see the good you also have to be willing to see how you are being hurtful.

A baby demands constant selfless giving from parents; a baby can push your "selfish buttons" like none other. You are forced to go against what you want in seemingly endless ways. Your baby feels your intentions, thoughts, and feelings especially when you suppress them. What a dilemma. You must love at your core. You can't pretend. You must be real and pure because babies don't relate to the superficial. It doesn't exist for them. They don't understand or acknowledge our pretenses until they become young children. Then they begin to learn our ways because they consider them to be an advantage. Unfortunately, *"our ways"* are only an advantage from a selfish perspective!

Our negative subconscious interactions are a monumental problem for our children. How we feel about them and how we treat them subconsciously affects them throughout their entire lifetimes. It can be a helpless feeling to see that you are hurting your child with your anger or selfishness because it is not always easy to change your reactive subconscious behavior, or to even consciously see exactly what you are doing. But, as painful as it may be to see and know you are perhaps doing harm to your infant or baby in the womb, a willingness to know is a huge step in the right direction.

Ignoring our subconscious does not make it go away. Unwillingness to see it does not make us better people. It's like if we don't see it, it doesn't exist. Or, I can't deal with this because I don't know how. I don't know where to start. Acknowledging these realities is a beginning point. With each new step, you will realize that it is possible. You have already started because the starting point is your desire and then your willingness to see the truth about yourself.

Willingness opens a door to an increasing ability to see and acknowledge the truth, whatever that truth may be. With each new step, you will have a new experience and find ways to change behaviors that you previously thought were impossible to change. It is a step-by-step process, and with each new step you will discover new truths and experiences. The subconscious is a world of psychic interaction that needs to be addressed and changed. Throughout this book I will relate many examples of subconscious control and hurtful interactions having to do with babies in the womb, infants, children, and adults.

Subconscious Memory: Your subconscious is where you automatically store every memory experience you have had since your conception. This is a record of what happened every second you were alive up until the present moment. Your every choice—intention, thought, feeling, and action—has been recorded by you subconsciously.

This is a full sensory memory record. When you access a memory here, you can remember what the day felt like, perhaps the smells, the colors, the people you were with, and the like. Sometimes we can remember accurately and relive the entire experience as it was in truth. This I would call your true memory. But, for most of us, most of the time, we remember our past with little edits to make it more pleasant, or unpleasant, or to make ourselves look better, or sometimes worse. Anyway, it is just not the whole truth. As I said, one step away from the truth, no true answers! In this instance no true you!

We all misuse our memories. Most of us have a *"script"* that we pull out and use when we talk to someone about ourselves. Somehow, our scripts always seem a better idea than the actual record. But, to the extent we do this we don't come across as real. Most of us get away with our scripts because they are usually not too far from the truth, so we don't notice each other using them. But, when we do this we don't touch; our scripts touch! Then we have those who are very noticeably accessing and elaborating on their *"scripts."* We usually call these people self-centered or obnoxious!

Unfortunately, there is yet another level: the crazy level. To varying degrees these people have distorted, not only the reality of their past, but also their present reality. The extreme is the schizophrenic, but then it goes the gamut of numerous dysfunctions right down to the level of normal, everyday people.

There was a study that claimed that most people do not recognize themselves when they catch a glimpse of themselves in a mirror. I found that fascinating because I have come to see that most of us don't really know ourselves at all! Haven't we all said at times, "*We are all crazy*"? When we say this, we are usually half kidding. However, it is true. We are all crazy to varying degrees. I would say that to the extent we are not honest and loving; we are crazy, because we are out of whack as a Human Being.

These days we seem to wear our dysfunctions as badges that we are proud of! We can do this because we believe that we are not at fault and are not responsible for our choices and behaviors, as incredible as that may seem, at least to me!

I personally believe that when we put medical names on people we dehumanize them. To us (and to them) they become what we have named them. They are a schizophrenic, or a manic-depressive, etc., etc. Not only that, the person him or herself uses the name as an excuse! I am manic-depressive. That is why I act the way I do. It is not my fault. It is because...whatever the reason! I know there is a reason, but I don't think that's it. I would say that dysfunctions have everything to do with conscious and subconscious choices to react negatively and destructively to various kinds and degrees of parental abuse, starting in the womb.

In many significant ways, we all keep reacting to our parents' negative choices in relation to us even after they have passed away. Not only that, as we grow older we project our reactions onto anyone in our immediate environment, especially our own children and family! As for our parents, if you think about it, there are no two people in the whole world that we have wanted more from. We expected true love from them; most often we did not get it. The sad fact is that, to varying degrees, we all use this truth as an excuse to negatively react, sometimes in the extreme and for an entire lifetime!

Because we all choose to be selfish and often control or strike-out in reaction to fulfill our desires to get even (or for a million other reasons) no one escapes the category of being *"an abuser."* Parental abuse begins with the enactment of subconscious selfish patterns and reactions that are projected onto a child in the womb and continues on, usually, throughout life.

This will be a fact as long as we are all choosing to enact negative subconscious intentions and patterns of thinking, feeling, and acting. This is what behavior is all about, not genes or anything else! This is quite a statement; however, with enough introspection you will see that it is true for you. We are all in the same boat here! According to the extent of our wrong conscious and subconscious intentions and choices, we will experience, to some degree, dysfunction and pain.

Maybe I have gotten a bit lengthy. Nonetheless, as long as we don't recognize how we are, and what we do subconsciously, our behaviors and lives will be a mystery and will pose a huge problem for us all. Our subconscious is not mysterious, and it is not very far away. You innately know how to process information and recall memories. Out of millions or trillions of bytes of memory, you know exactly where to find what you are looking for: perhaps the name of a grade-school friend, or someone's phone number. When you think about it, this is a tremendous feat.

Unfortunately, there is much that we don't want to remember. That makes remembering in general more difficult. Honesty is a key factor here. You have to be consciously willing to see the truth to retrieve accurately a memory. To run from a painful or embarrassing past is disastrous. You can never truly heal unless you are willing to face the truth and accept it. You may find that you are running from seeing and accepting the truth about your own wrong choices that were in reaction to a nightmarish past. As you become more honest and willing to acknowledge the actual truth consciously, you will be able to access more easily memories that have become subconscious. When you continue on this path, your subconscious will no longer be a mysterious element of your being. You will get to see some amazing aspects of yourself.

You have an entire life on the subconscious level of your being. But to get there you will have to see and accept many negatives about yourself. The joke is that you already know all the bad. You are the one who buried it there in the first place. It takes courage; it takes work, but it is well worth the effort.

Subconscious Control of Bodily Functions: Everything about your physical body, all your complicated bodily functions such as heart rate, breathing, and a seemingly endless list of functions, is actually controlled and regulated by you subconsciously. You, the being, the Human Being, are overseeing and making your body work. I can't really tell you how we do all of this; I wish I knew a clairvoyant medical doctor. I'll bet he or she could give us a wealth of information about this process.

In ending this chapter, I would like to share with you some scientific medical research facts about unborn babies. Our lives begin in the womb. We have amazing abilities starting at a very young age. But to acknowledge this, and to study what our choices may have been in the womb, would require a commitment of responsibility for our behavior. That, alas, is a level of responsibility that most of us avoid.

Here are some facts taken from medical scientific studies on babies in the womb. Many additional facts can be found on the Internet.

- *Unborn babies make choices, think, feel, remember, hear, learn, and react in positive or negative ways.*

- *Unborn babies can discern subtle differences in their mother's attitudes and feelings and can be observed responding to them.*

- *Unborn babies display patterns of fear or anger that are visible using ultrasound. These behavior patterns are usually replicated after birth and during infancy.*

- *Unborn babies sense and react to not only strong negative emotions such as intense fear, anger, or hate, but also much subtler feelings such as uncertainty, insecurity, anxiety, and frustration.*

- *Unborn babies, by the time they are ready to be born, have distinctive, observable personalities.*

- *Ultrasound images of twins in the womb show them expressing feelings. They will repeatedly hit, kick, hug, kiss, and play together.*

- *The unexpressed psychological state of a pregnant woman is crucial to the mental, emotional, and physical well-being of her unborn baby.*

- *Studies on schizophrenic and psychotic pregnant women and their babies show the terrible psychological effects that extreme negative mental and emotional energies can have on an unborn baby.*

- *A mother's attitude had the greatest effect on how her baby turned out. Women, who consciously and subconsciously wanted their babies, had the easiest pregnancies and births. They also tended to have the healthiest children, both physically and emotionally.*

- *A father's attitude is significant. Fathers who make choices to control, own, or possess their babies emit consistently coercive and hurtful energies that are disturbing and painful to their unborn babies.*

In looking at our parents (and our reactions to them) we can determine what our responses and reactions might have been while we were in the womb and thereafter. To get a sense of what our experiences were and our choices, either in reaction or response, to the behaviors of our parents would be a giant step in understanding our destructive intentions, drives, and choices in general.

Starting in the womb, it was our own reactive choices to the choices of our parents and others that have imbedded us in our negative behavior. When we understand this thoroughly, changing our subconscious behavior becomes possible. With understanding sincere willingness can become a reality within us. With sincere willingness, substantial change is just around the corner! Changing in loving ways then becomes a lifelong endeavor because we understand the essence of what it means to be a truly genuine Human Being.

Understanding can be the key that unlocks the door to our basic willingness to do what is truly right, loving, honest, and lovingly responsible. Changing our subconscious negative intentions and selfishness would also be an insurance that our children will not become at the effect of our subconscious destructive choices. To know ourselves on our deepest subconscious levels is the beginning of true inner understanding, healing, and substantial loving change.

Two
Our Human Beginnings

"If we could consciously tap into our earliest memory records, we would remember and see exactly how our physical bodies developed inside the womb."

In this chapter, I will narrate (in the second person) an unborn baby's experience. I will cite scientific studies that relate to the physical, the mental, and the emotional development of a baby in utero. I will use my own clairvoyant research to detail and expand on (with excerpts in quotes and italics) the psychological lives of individual babies in the womb, newborns, and infants, as well as their parents.

At conception, you are an intelligent being who possesses the ability to be aware and to choose. You have a subconscious awareness of self; awareness that you are an *"I,"* the way you are now consciously aware that you are an *"I."*

I found this amazing statement on a reputable site on the Internet: *"The roots of human behavior, researchers now know, begin to develop early—just weeks after conception, in fact."*

"At the exact moment, the sperm penetrated the egg, there was an explosion of light. That explosion was the beginning of a new human life. The life had a primitive experience of self. The light consisted of white and blue energies. I interpreted the white energy as intuitive knowing; the blue energy as innate intelligence. These were psychological aspects of the embryo."

"The embryo looks transparent and almost liquid but is becoming more solid. I observed what appeared to be a primitive awareness and an impulse to live and survive. In this tiny consciousness, I sensed not only the desire to live, but also, an awareness of the possible danger of loss of life. I experienced these two impulses in the embryo as a desire for independence and a quickening sense of fear of potential loss. The impulses seemed to be coming from the embryo's will and awareness, which were the essential elements of his primitive consciousness and being."

Every embryo I've read possessed a will that seemed essentially no different from the will of an adult. I sensed that embryos were capable of a full primitive psychological experience of life. The awareness of self was coming from a basic knowledge that he or she was alive. *"I am seeing the spark of consciousness as orange and blue. The blue light is the embryo's consciousness and the orange is her* *mother's energy on her. She wanted to make this pregnancy happen. She felt she was creating this baby by her intention, but she was only allowing the embryo to live by her intention."*

At the outset, in a primitive way, you are beginning to make choices; you are responding and reacting to your physical and psychological energetic environments. You, the being, the Human Being, are orchestrating the intelligence of the DNA. With your intelligence and will, you are directing the physical development of your cells as well as directing every aspect of your physical body.

"The embryo is growing rapidly, and her consciousness is enclosed within her. There is a sense of quiet and being hidden. She seems to be dormant, but at the same time, is experiencing the growth activity of her physical body cells. She is so small and so enclosed inside that it seems that her consciousness is not there. Nonetheless, she is experiencing an extremely primitive life in the growth of the initial stages of her body. When I saw her waking up around the eighth week, she was beginning to reference herself to her boundaries."

"From what I am seeing now, her consciousness is experiencing something minute and integral. She seems to always have been conscious of the particular stages of development she has been experiencing and participating in."

Previously I would report embryos as coming awake when they reached a certain stage of development. That was because at a more mature stage a baby's consciousness had become more visible to me.

You, the being, the Human Being, are manifesting through each and every cell. You are focusing your will and awareness within each cell that is growing according to the genetic plan. Your presence in each cell is giving life; without it your cells would die.

"Between three and four weeks: The embryo is still minute. He looks like he is being formed from the inside of each cell. This tiny mass is being shaped from within."

"I'm seeing that the embryo is starting to be aware of his inner functions such as certain physical organs being formed."

"When reading an embryo only three weeks old, I saw her energetically resisting and fighting for her life when her mother was seriously considering an abortion. Even before this embryo appeared to be consciously aware of her mother's existence, she seemed to be energetically pleading for her life and fearing her death. The embryo's reaction was occurring without any observable exchange of thoughts or images. The reaction came from an innate knowledge that she was alive and that her life was in danger. If this seems absurd, it is not. Think of any

living creature from the smallest to the largest; all will fight to stay alive or will run or squirm at the possibility of death."

"A woman who previously had two miscarriages and was now pregnant again: The mother desperately wanted to keep this baby. The embryo was energetically communicating with her mother by her willingness to live. The mother was willing the baby to stay and grow. The baby and mother's joint willingness was moving the pregnancy through places of potential danger where certain hook-ups might have been weak or flawed."

During the initial stages, an embryo body faces numerous potential obstacles. Millions of connections must be made perfectly. The first few weeks of life are crucial. It is surprising how many healthy babies are born given all that might go wrong in this extremely complex and precise physical progression. An attitude of willingness is required by the embryo and mother for those connections to be successful and for the baby to live and grow. This cooperation is an important factor in psychological and physical development.

In three weeks' time your heart has started to beat. By six weeks you are rotating your arms, legs, and head.

Your physical movements are showing whether you are feeling comfortable or uncomfortable, also, your movements are giving you a sense that you are separate from your environment.

"The baby seems to be very active and is moving around a lot. She is discovering that the more she moves, the better she feels."

"During the eighth week, the baby is being enveloped in his mother's religious ideas. The physical growth energy is more basic than the mother's psychological energies. The natural growth energies seem to have the power to clear the baby's body and aura of outside interference. The mother keeps putting her energies on her baby, but they keep getting pushed out by the natural growth energy.

I'm seeing greens, yellows, and blues in and around the embryo. These are natural energies. Nonetheless, I have seen that soon when the embryo body is more developed and stable the growth energy seems to have stopped that process of clearing the body and aura."

"Between two and a half to three months in the womb: Before the twins are showing any physical signs of being aware of themselves, they are extremely aware of each other. There is a kind of comfort here—a sense of comfort in having the presence of the other near. They are learning from each other.

They are learning by the presence of the other somehow—following each other, copying one another. There is very definitely a connection and a companionship here. It has to do with a sensing or psychic experience."

You have developed a feeling sense and are conscious that you are alive. This is the beginning of your conscious awareness of your physical body and physical development.

"At eight weeks: The fetus baby is enjoying his mother's physical energies. Because of her excellent physical health and active lifestyle he is feeling a sense of physical stability. He is energized and feels good. His consciousness is coming awake more and more. He is growing and developing in a yellow light and he's feeling himself growing. He's experiencing himself energetically. I don't see that he is thinking per se, but he is somehow involved in the process of growth that he is going through."

I'm including the following excerpts because these kinds of energetic bombardments are common. To the extent that a mother (or father) is dysfunctional or even just unstable, her (or his) unborn baby is sure to suffer. Knowing this could help a pregnant mother (and father) attempt to curtail her (or his) *"craziness"* for the sake of their baby.

"There is restriction going on in this physical growth process. The mother is being consciously and subconsciously destructive. Her selfish choices are hindering her baby's normal physical growth."

Drinking alcohol, smoking, eating poorly, and psychic attacks are some ways a pregnant woman will hurt her baby's physical progress.

"This mother has many destructive and self-destructive patterns; so, it is taking a strong willingness on the part of the embryo to attain her necessary physical development. The embryo is making choices every step of the way."

If a mother is feeling invaded by the embryo or feels put upon by the "inconvenience" of being pregnant, she will do hurtful things to her baby. This mother is telling herself that a couple of beers will not hurt anything. She is also eating excessive amounts of sugar and this weakens the embryo's body and physical growth process in a real way.

"The baby's father is hiding his feelings of excitement and jealousy. He is afraid that his wife will react to his excitement and deprive him of access to the baby or make him jealous by making herself special to the baby."

Fathers may become jealous and feel left out of what they perceive as a "mother-child loving bond," which is usually not what is going on at all.

When a person is expressing love in a right way you will feel love and inclusion, not left out and jealous. We have so many intertwined patterns that we enact on a regular basis. To lessen or eliminate our inner struggles we need to make choices to stop acting selfishly. We do this by choosing to do what is right in the exact situation in which we are having the problem.

I have often seen fathers who are genuinely happy about their babies coming. Babies can feel this, and they respond in positive ways. So, my point is that fathers, when sincerely caring for and loving their unborn babies, can have their own special moments in a right and good way. Both parents should strive for a genuine, loving connection with their baby. This requires consistent and sustained selfless choices.

"The way her husband interacts with the children makes her feel inadequate. He is outgoing and giving. Nonetheless, she thinks he is indifferent because he does not have the negative emotional ties that she experiences with the children. She feels the family is like a part-time job for him. The mother is also beginning to be threatened by the baby being a girl. She is jealous at the thought of her husband making her little girl special to him. She does not want her daughter to be first with him."

As silly as this appears, I find it is quite common for women to feel this way. Many women have deep competition patterns with other females.

"The embryo is ten weeks old. The mother's angry energy is coercive and is inhibiting the embryo's natural progress. The mother feels she had to have this baby and is blaming the baby. She is panicked that the baby is taking her life away, that her baby is drawing life from her and she is becoming less. She is creating this mental and emotional trauma because

she feels that she does not want the baby."

The mother's dysfunction stems from past sexual abuse by her father that she has suppressed. Becoming pregnant has lit up those traumatic memories that she is not willing to consciously acknowledge; so, she is making up several irrational scenarios to explain (to herself) her craziness. The baby's father is humiliated that his girlfriend is pregnant and they are not yet married; they've been together for years. She is embarrassed to tell people because she says that she is not the mother type.

"This woman is a waitress and she thought people at work would judge her for being pregnant and not married. At four months, she is beginning to show and is now committed to having the baby. People are congratulating her. She is surprised and happy with their responses. She's feeling good about herself and about having the baby. I'm sure the baby feels good energies at this moment!"

There are so many moments in time! When we make right choices in each new moment what a relief it is! When you're feeling down on yourself or discouraged, there is always that next moment to make a right choice. Every moment is always *"just a moment in time."* When we use our moments wisely we can climb out of any hole we find ourselves in, no matter how desperate we feel, or how deep the hole.

An important point: Even though this mother was sometimes thinking about abortion, the embryo was not affected by her thoughts because she never actually had an intention to abort. On the other hand, a woman can say she wants her baby, but she really does not. If this hidden stance is not acknowledged and changed, it will become a painful nightmare for her unborn baby.

An example of the trauma of an unborn child when the mother does not want the baby but decides to keep him or her:

"At five weeks, this mother has decided to keep her baby. However, she is still trying to abort her child subconsciously. The embryo is somehow aware and holding his own, without any signs of being conscious. I sense a solid heaviness and a determination to stay.

At three months, there is a sensation of wanting to cry. *He is feeling overwhelmed and a strong downward pull from his mother's depression. At five months, he is experiencing noises and external energies as adversaries. He is constantly on-edge and has become distrustful. His anxious stance is distorting his perceptions. His prior inwardness has been replaced by nervous activity and agitation.*

The birth*: When the contractions started he was mentally hiding while having to yield to the physical birthing process.*

He felt that both the anesthesia and birth were being imposed upon him. *Immediately after birth he felt relief. The nurses had positive energies and he felt secure in their presence. When he was brought to his mother he was asleep and afraid to wake up. The predominant physical feeling was one of being drugged. The underlying emotional feeling was despairing at being alone and fearing what might lie ahead. This woman appeared to be a good mother with two other children. The couple was affluent, and seemed happy with no obvious problems."*

By the eighth week movement has become your major way of discovery. You are becoming increasingly aware of yourself by your continued movements.

At every turn, you are discovering new realities in your environment.

"The fetus is still very small. She seems to be straight, not curled up and her arms and legs are moving. The fetus is growing fast. She is absolutely recording experience as she goes along. It is as if she is experiencing and watching the process, and there seems to be a kind of natural involvement."

"At two months in the womb the twins are aware of each other by a sonar-like ability. Sonar: 'A method for detecting and locating objects submerged in water by means of the sound of waves they reflect or produce.' They are extremely physically aware of each other as persons and as entities even before they are physically

aware of their mother."

"Twin boys at three months: Tom is amazed that this other presence is there right close to him. I'm seeing them having a bond between them, an acknowledgement that each one is there, an energetic bond or agreement to be together, to be with one another and to be there for one another. This is all on a willing, energetic level—no mental or emotional awareness that I can see. There is the sense that they are the same— they are bonded together in this situation that they're in."

For the past while you have been moving almost constantly. You have discovered your hands and feet. You are realizing that the fluid you are shooting around in is not you; it is not a part of your consciousness and body. You know that you are separate from it. You are becoming very clear about your physical boundaries.

"A twin at ten weeks: The baby has already energetically connected with his mother, being basically angry. He is energetically agreeing to be as his mother wants him to be. He is extremely aware of his brother next to him. They both seem to be shooting around and aware of their boundaries and aware of their physical separateness in relation to one another."

By twelve weeks, your major physical organs are developed enough to be visible. You have begun regular cycles of activity and rest. By fifteen weeks, you are moving in response to your mother's laughs or coughs. You can taste the difference between sweet, bitter, and sour. You are now making purposeful movements, such as sucking your thumb, in an effort to calm yourself when you are stressed or threatened. You are also gradually beginning to hear faint sounds that are drawing your attention outward. These amazing abilities were observable by medical scientists using ultrasound.

"Twin boys: Dennis is very present at three months. He is almost explosively present. He can't stand what he feels from his mother. He's moving around, feeling his body and his womb space. Craig feels like he is straining. He is inward and kind of just there, like a dull sense of awareness, an absence of being present in his body and womb space. Dennis is going from hugging Craig to pushing him away. He's not getting the response he wants from his brother so he is trying different things. He is trying to get Craig to recognize that he is there next to him. Craig is extremely inward and is not responding."

At four months, you are now clearly able to hear sounds. This is a great psychological happening. It is a *"eureka"* moment. Throughout your time in the womb you will have many of these eureka moments which will continue through infancy. Amazingly, you are putting the pieces of your puzzle together; and as you do, you are becoming ever more aware.

I would like to point out that as in life, so it is in the womb. Events don't just happen automatically. Typically, our experience depends greatly on our previous understanding and choices, that is, how we have used our awareness and will during our time so far. At around four months babies are physically able to hear. Generally, this is true, however a baby's experience depends on what has been impacting him or her, and how the baby has been responding. Consequently, each baby may have a delayed or a different experience of hearing. This experience involves both physical and emotional issues.

Some babies at four months in the womb:

"His physical ears are now developed. His ability to hear has gradually become acute. It is as if he was previously sleeping and is slowly waking to various sounds. He is listening now to sounds that are soothing to him. I think they are musical tones. However, he does not hear the whole song, just certain notes at a certain pitch. They are very pleasing. I think I am observing this baby listening to classical music—perhaps, a piano or a harp. Someone in his environment might be playing the instrument. The fetus seems content within himself."

"There is a sense of confusion. This fetus can hear sounds, but he is not clear about what is happening around him, or what he is experiencing."

Development is not clear-cut: Understanding depends much on the fetus' positive or negative environment. His environment is usually a little of both; but, all too often, it can be a consistently negative one.

"Four months one week: He is moving his legs and kicking, but I still do not see his attention going out. This is not good."

"He is afraid of the sounds around him. He is feeling harsh and hurtful energies and has not yet discovered where they are coming from."

"She is hearing sounds now. Her mother plays soothing music and she can hear her mother's voice, which lately sounds frustrated and irritated. Her mother is trying to restrain her anger regarding her son; but he drives her crazy. She thinks that it is his age that is making him so aggressive."

I'm using examples of twins because two babies in the womb show us just how smart and developed we all are at such a young age.

"Twins at four months: The babies seem small for their age. I'm tuning into the basically angry fetus, Gwen. I'm not seeing her hearing yet, but Grace is beginning to hear with kind of an echo. She's slightly more developed than her sister and is hearing sooner. I'm looking to see when the basically angry fetus, Gwen, is beginning to hear—somewhere between four and four-and-a-half months. The first thing that

she's recognizing is her mother's heartbeat. This is comforting to her. I'm seeing Gwen swaying or moving to the heartbeat.

The basically fearful fetus, Grace, is hearing before Gwen, but she's not understanding as much because she's still inward and she's not being drawn out by sounds. Grace is hearing sounds, but she not following them to investigate. But Gwen is following the sounds and investigating and interacting with them, like this swaying and moving to the mother's heartbeat."

"Twins at four months: Hank and Barry have a strong energetic connection. I'm seeing Barry poking Hank trying to get him to come out of his shell and interact. Hank is staying pretty much to himself, although he's extremely aware of what's happening with Barry. He's also very aware of the communication that Barry has with his parents: the psychic mental and feeling communication. These two babies are so involved with each other that it's not like reading a single fetus who is communicating with both parents. Here the interactions with the parents seem to be secondary to the life that the twins are living together in the womb."

With your newly acquired ability to hear you are now able to solve many prior mysteries. You now realize that there is a world outside of your immediate womb environment. You are making the connection that much of the irritating and sometimes painful energies that you had been experiencing were not an essential part you. This realization is primarily in relation to your mother. She is your first discovery. Even though you are inside her body you are experiencing her energy as distinctly different from your own. You are becoming aware of your mother's voice and heartbeat. You are becoming familiar with and, amazingly, you are memorizing the voices of both your mother and father, which you will recognize when tested after birth.

"The fetus is at the effect of his mother's negative thoughts and feelings which are creating an atmosphere of restlessness. When she is feeling good and making right choices, the fetus experiences a sense of relief."

"At times, the baby feels the lightness and pleasure of his mother's contentment. However, these are just passing moments. The mother's underlying state is one of stress because of her choices to focus on and worry about herself, rather than to truly care about her pregnancy and her unborn baby."

You are gaining continued evidence that there are things apart from you. Previously you were experiencing outside emotions as your own. Now you realize that they are different from you; you are recognizing what is essential to you and what is foreign. You see that the energies of your mother and father are coming at you; they are not a part of you.

They are coming from outside.

"At five months, I am seeing extensive control energy on the baby. It is coming from the father. He is reacting to the fuss his wife is making over the baby. It annoys him and makes him angry. A deeper reason for his desire to possess this child is that the baby has gone into subconscious negative agreement with her mother. He imagines they have a special bond and he feels left out.

This father's major annoyance is that his wife, over the months of the pregnancy, has withdrawn from him and has had most of her attention on herself and the baby. She has been feeling that the baby would be a compatible relationship to fulfill her in ways her husband could not. He is reading her thoughts subconsciously and is severely reacting to what she is thinking."

You visibly respond when a bright light is shone on the outside of your mother's stomach. Some babies move toward the light and fixate on it, others move away from the light disturbed by it. In reacting to the light, you are showing your ability to see objects in space and respond to them in a determined and coordinated way.

"The baby is hearing sounds and playing with her thumbs and fingers. She is gaining understanding. She is acknowledging different colors. Her mother goes up and down and the baby rides on her feeling

rollercoaster."

You are in an amazing and precise process of discovery. You have taken a quantum leap in awareness by suddenly becoming aware of the outside world. With this realization, you are fast becoming more psychologically complex.

"Even though the baby is afraid of venturing out, she is exploring and moving about in the womb. She is exploring her hands and feet and exploring with body movements. She seems to be mostly in her own world and ignoring the energies of her mother, yet feeling restricted by them. As the baby gets bigger, her mother believes she is getting more excited about the baby being a girl. But, really, she is anxious, nervous, irritated, and agitated."

"The baby is kicking and moving a lot. The movement helps the pressure she experiences when her mother smokes. She is isolated and alone and is afraid to reach out to her father. She feels enclosed and restricted by her mother and sorry for herself. She is experiencing her mother's feelings of depression and aloneness as if they were her own."

These discoveries have also presented to you an entirely new psychological arena in which you will interact. You are now rapidly developing mentally and emotionally; you are becoming a well-defined Human Being months before you are born. During your short life, you have learned much about energies and are about to learn much more.

You are now gradually gaining the ability to see and understand the psychic mental and emotional thoughts and feelings of your parents and other family members. You can clairvoyantly read your mother and father's true intentions, thoughts, feelings, and psychic energetic actions. You know when positive or negative energies are directed toward you. At times you suddenly (a *"eureka"* moment) understand the mental and emotional attitudes of your parents and how they feel about you in a certain moment or during a specific time.

"The baby is looking out reading energies and thoughts. She feels tied to her mother but is afraid of her mother's energy. The mother has lessened her desperate hold on the baby, and this is helping the baby to look at her mother's thoughts. Nonetheless, she is still afraid to reach out to her father because her mother hits her with jealous energy when she does.

I am getting a choking sensation again. This has something to do with the mother's demands. She will not allow the fetus to express. When the fetus reaches out energetically to the boys (her siblings) or to her father, her mother restricts her with energy. I am seeing the choking sensation is more emotional than physical."

As you are developing your clairvoyant and communication skills, you are reacting or responding

to your parents' intentions, attitudes, demands, expectations, thoughts, feelings, and their energetic atmospheres in general. At times, you are feeling negative energies that are emotionally and sometimes physically painful. You are also experiencing loving energies that are soothing and reassuring.

"This mother was seven months pregnant when I met her. To look at her you would think her baby would be very healthy, but her child is in pain. She drinks, smokes, and takes drugs on occasion. This womb baby is in trauma. The way the mother looks and acts is dramatically different from her inner and hidden experience and that of her baby. The baby is rigid because he does not feel safe. He is dizzy much of the time and his skin is sore.

He is energetically going out toward his father who is soft and real. The baby seems to be in agreement with him. He is watching him and copying him. The baby has a sister who is communicating with him also. He keeps his attention out to connect with them. He cannot do that while going inward. He is depending on his father's attention and acceptance to feel secure. He follows him with attention wherever he goes. This is often an escape and a distraction for the baby. His presence is not in his body and his focus is not on his growth and womb space as it should be. The baby is emotionally running from his circumstances.

Having his attention out is positive only when he is not avoiding reality. When his attention is on his father to avoid the experience with his mother, he will not see either one in truth. This is something that many children do; it is a pattern that begins in the womb."

The more a person stays solidly in his or her body, the more active and healthy he or she will be at any age. The physical body needs that presence to function and grow properly.

"The baby's attachment to his father started at four months and has been getting stronger ever since. The mother is taking this as a rejection, which it is. She is jealous and has put gray energy over the baby, but he persists and keeps putting his attention on his father. In reaction, she is withdrawing and not caring. This puts the baby in a lot of fear. He is and will be at the mercy of her choices. She can cause him pain and he is well-aware of that."

You are now beginning to act in positive and negative ways in response to the kinds of energies being directed to you. You are observing, feeling, and reacting to the mental and emotional energies in your immediate environment, that is, your parents and siblings. When there is chaos, fighting or suppressed negative thoughts, feelings, or psychic actions; you are experiencing the specific energies involved. When your surroundings are filled with love and caring intentions, thoughts, feelings, and psychic and physical actions, you feel content and reassured.

When you negatively reacted to your parents' hurtful energies is when you began to create your own negative patterns of behavior. Your awareness and communication, at this point, are totally psychic and energetic. Because of this you feel most everything that is going on with your parents and siblings. In other words, you will respond, or react and be affected by your environment, even though you are still in your mother's womb.

You are discovering that you can send thought and picture images to your parents and siblings. You are learning to do this from your parents and siblings who are sending you messages when they are thinking about you or feeling certain ways about you. These communications are mental and emotional telepathy.

Most parents are not aware that they are, in fact, communicating. It is usually more of a belief than knowledge of the interaction. Yet, I have seen some young siblings consciously interact.

"While her mother was doing laundry, a girl, about four years old, was sitting drinking a soda and looking calm and content. I saw that she was communicating with her brother in the womb. She was feeling good about him soon to be born and was looking forward to playing with him. There were light yellow and pink energies going back and forth between them. The yellow energy was expression and pink a loving

feeling."

By the time you are five months in the womb you have become adept at regular energetic communications with your parents and siblings. Brainwave tests can pick up your periods of REM sleep. This indicates a dream state, and dreaming signifies thinking and the processing of images that have meaning to you. While you are sleeping your facial expression and body movement show whether you are having a pleasant or an unpleasant sleep experience.

You listen all the time. Scientists can observe your body dancing to the rhythm of your mother's voice, and also to music. At first, you are startled by a loud noise, but in time you learn to discriminate and ignore certain routine noises in your surroundings.

"Twins at five months: The twins seem to be bigger and healthier. They've grown a lot in one month. Gwen is moving a lot, tumbling, moving, and communicating with her mother. It doesn't seem that the mother consciously knows yet that she has twins. Gwen interacts with her mother and is feeling secure in that connection.

Grace the basically fearful fetus is copying her sister—darting around, tumbling, and moving. She has discovered her mother's heartbeat because her sister was moving to the rhythm of the mother's heartbeat, and Grace was moving to the rhythm of her sister, and then she connected her moving to this boom-boom, boom-boom that she was hearing—the heartbeat. In this way Grace is making connections and learning things through her sister."

You are shaping your attitudes, character, and personality by how you choose to respond to what you are feeling and perceiving. By your choices in response, or in reaction to your parents' intentions, attitudes, demands, and positive and negative energies you are shaping your character. When you react negatively you are strengthening your basic approach to life (angry or fearful). You are also strengthening your agreements and patterns that you have taken on essentially from one parent.

Choice of Disposition:

"At three months in the womb the baby is energetically going into negative agreement with her mother. The mother is basically fearful, and the baby will be basically fearful. When I sensed this fetus being drawn to her mother I realized that the fetus had made a choice to be basically fearful thus the connection with her basically fearful mother. This happening became clearer with each new fetus reading."

Negative Agreement: "The baby has already gone into basic negative agreement with his mother. He has agreed to control his expression and be as she wants him to be. He does not know what this means yet, but he is agreeing with her energetically."

These agreements will affect his relationship with his father and have other serious ramifications for him. This type of child-to-parent negative agreement is common. I have seen it happen with literally every person I have read so far.

Negative Agreement: "From about the seventh month on, the fetus was entering into mental and emotional agreements with his mother because he sensed she would help him get what he wanted and needed as he went through life."

He senses that he does not have control over his environment or the people around him. Because of this, he feels helpless. Because of his sense of helplessness, he believes that agreements with his mother are necessary.

Negative Agreement: "The baby is reading how her mother feels about men and is already choosing to take-on some of her mother's ideas about men and how they are."

Negative Agreement: "This mother blames her lack of care on being tired because she is pregnant and has to care for three other children. Her husband resents her and feels jealous and left out. His jealousy stems from his subconscious knowledge that his baby has gone into negative agreement with his wife."

Negative Agreement: "The fetus is aligning herself with her mother's ideas and energy. She is deciding to be angry and aggressive like her mother and is withdrawing from her father's energy."

Negative Agreement: "The fetus is basically angry and going out toward his basically angry father. The mother is basically fearful and is insecure. The baby is now afraid to be in agreement with his father. When he energetically reaches out to his father his mother hits him with angry energy. This is a pattern that she also enacts with her husband (she hits him with angry energy) whenever he looks at another woman. She feels she just cannot tolerate that. She consciously knows she is afraid that, after the baby is born, her husband will steal the baby's affections."

A fetus begins making agreements at about three months. At three months, he or she does not have agreements in words or pictures. That will come later. The unborn baby's experience of an agreement is like a bonding sense. The fetus somehow knows, and feels a demand to be however that parent wants him or her to be and accepts, usually reluctantly. However, the baby always perceives some potential benefit.

A parent can experience his or her instigation of an agreement by acknowledging desires for the baby to have specific traits, or to be like or not like him or her. These agreements are hurtful. They can also be so tricky! You may only be barely conscious, or not at all conscious, that it is not right to want your child to be certain ways, especially if they are positive ways. The only approach to deal with this dilemma is to work on being as unselfish as you can possibly be—not an easy task!

Since you have innate awareness of rightness and love, you know that how you choose, at this totally young age, is the most important challenge you face. You innately know that you have the abilities of awareness and choice. You know that, at every moment, you must choose one way or the other. You innately know that you always have the option to respond in a loving way to the negativity you may be experiencing.

On a happier note, when your mother or father is genuinely caring about you, it is a great support. A truly loving parent will nurture you in mental, emotional, and physical ways. True and selfless caring makes it so much easier for you to make the right choices necessary for you to have a healthy mental, emotional, and physical experience, while you are in the womb and for the rest of your life!

Having read over this chapter there seem to be two concerns. The first concern is: "Could I have been one of those parents who energetically hurt my unborn child without even knowing it?" The short answer is, if you were making selfish choices, yes. I would say for all of us the answer is "*yes*" to varying degrees because we all choose to be hurtful and selfish at times, often without even consciously knowing it.

The second concern is from you as a fetus: *"How could I have known to make right choices in an environment and atmosphere with possibly so much hurtful negativity and uncertainty? I was only a fetus."*

The short answer is, the same way that you know now. At each moment, you have a choice to make. You must be aware of that. You are the same being, the same Human Being, that you were then. You made the same choices for or against rightness, truth, love, and loving responsibility as you are doing at this moment.

Ironically, we make selfish choices thinking they are to our benefit. We do this now, and we did it when we were babies in the womb. As you can see the womb environment can be an extremely difficult place in which to make unselfish choices. We seem to be at the mercy of our parents. However, that is not true. The more right choices we made in the womb, the more we came to realize the truth of our situation. The more right choices we made, the better our experience. *That* never changes!

We were always in control of our most basic abilities, to be aware of rightness and to act on it. When we did, we had an immediate positive change of experience. It was quite a test (metaphorically) that none of us have passed with flying colors. Incidentally, the same principle is true now. The more right choices we make, the more we realize that we are totally at cause within the universe of ourselves.

The long answer to both questions involves all our excuses and lies that have made us so complicated. We pretend and come to believe that we are not the extraordinary beings that we truly are. How crazy is that?!

It leads us to ask questions like, *"How do I know what is actually right, true, loving, and lovingly responsible?"* Within ourselves and in our immediate environments we always know the right, honest, loving and responsible action to take. When we deny this, we are denying the truth of our basic humanness. This denial sets us off in an extremely complicated direction. To assume such a substantial lie makes it literally impossible to come to the truth of who we are. In our immediate inner and outer life, we always know what is right and true!

When we have come so far away from the truth about ourselves it may take some work to get back there; but, essentially and subconsciously, we always know the truth of <u>who</u> we are and <u>how</u> we are. We all know when we are lying. What are we lying in relation to? The truth of course!

In the last few decades we have developed a new perspective on the truth. You have your *"truth"*, and I have my *"truth."* Very convenient! We used to say, *"You have your opinion, and I have my opinion."* That, at least, assumes that, outside of both of our opinions, there is an actual truth. That assumption seems to no longer exist, at least in the way we present our realities. This selfcentered shift in perspective represents a huge problem in our society today.

Remember when you were a child. All children know right from wrong, when they are lying or telling the truth. They know when they are being loved and when they are not; they know their childhood responsibilities. They also know when they are being nice, or not nice, when they are being mean, or caring about another child. They certainly know when they are being defiant.

How you respond to what is coming at you determines your character and personality. Your character and personality define the essential quality and direction of your life. This never changes; it is always true no matter how young or old you are, and no matter what your individual circumstances.

As far as our innate abilities are concerned we are all equal. To know and choose for right intentions, and to make loving choices, are actions we can all take when we are willing. Believe it or not, no matter who you are, no matter what your past circumstances were, or what you may possess, you will always experience the immediate good or bad effects of your choices.

Three
Forming Your Character

"Medical research studies demonstrate that unborn babies, by the time they are ready to be born, have distinctive, observable personalities."

At only five months in the womb, you now have many more decisions to make. These will dramatically affect your experience in the womb and for the rest of your life. You are forming your character by your basic choices for good or for bad, for right or for wrong, for loving or for selfish.

You are now halfway through your time in the womb and you are becoming more mature in every way. You are still kicking and flexing your muscles and testing out your reflexes. You have also been listening to the sounds of blood rushing around, your lungs working, and your heart beating. These are the exact activities you should be focusing on during this time.

"This baby seems to be growing increasingly aware of himself, and of himself as regards to his outer

world. I'm seeing that he continues to experience his physical boundaries using his hands, feet, and body. He seems to have an awareness that his consciousness is within his body looking out, even though his eyes are not yet open. His consciousness is looking out in an energetic feeling sensing kind of way."

You have now become able to see energies and can distinguish between different energies by color and feel. You can see and understand the thoughts and emotions contained in those energies, that is, what the energies mean essentially. You are now becoming able to accurately identify various intentions, thoughts, and feelings. In a hostile environment you see dark reds, dark purples, and other strong colors. You are discovering that what you are feeling and understanding matches the energetic colors you are seeing. At each step, you have something new to figure out.

If this seems unreasonable think of a newborn, infant, or toddler; they are constantly discovering and learning. Doesn't it make sense that they didn't just begin this activity at birth?

Strong, dark colors are angry, hostile, and willful energies. The lighter, happier, loving energies are yellow, pink, and other pastel colors. You are discovering that you are extremely sensitive to both the loving and hurtful energies. You know that the lighter energies have a pleasant secure feel, while the darker energies are harsh and painful. Your understanding of this entire dynamic depends upon how much you are willing to see life as it is and respond as you innately know you should.

As in life, so it is in the womb. As unbelievable and challenging as this may appear, seeing the truth and making right and loving choices in response to negativity will bring a sense of both psychical and psychological security. Not acting rightly creates all kinds of complicated behavior patterns that begin and are reinforced while we are still in the womb.

You now weigh about one pound and are ten to twelve inches long. Your body is proportional to your arms and legs, balancing out your head. Your features, including your eyes and ears, are in their final position and have begun functioning. You are developing eyebrows. Even your fingernails, toenails, and the hair on your scalp are growing. You also have your own unique fingerprints.

"He seems to be distinguishing himself from his mother and his surroundings. He somehow knows that the sack of fluid he is moving in is not him. He knows that the fluid is not a part of his consciousness and body. He knows that he is separate from it. The more he grows and develops the more conscious and aware he seems to become of himself and his circumstances. His feeling level is also becoming greater. He just keeps becoming increasingly aware and more mentally and emotionally alive. I'm seeing this happening, yet

I don't know how it is happening. It appears that the fetus is using some part of his brain in some way."

An ultrasound shows your hands, which open and close freely. Your parents can finally opt to know if you are a boy or a girl. You look much like you will at birth. Although you appear to be fully formed, you still have plenty of maturation ahead of you. The most important maturing at this point is your mental and emotional development.

"The baby is sending messages to his oldest sister who is curious about him. She is hoping for a little brother, and she talks to him as her brother."

"The fetus has stability and is more solid with a kind of physical certainty that she is going to be healthy."

"The baby seems active, alert, is looking out, and has her attention outward. She has put her attention on her father, wanting communication. The father is now responding to his baby and willing to put positive attention on her. The father does not know that he is actually communicating; he does know that he feels love for his unborn child and wants to care for her."

Again, when a father (or mother) is willing to communicate with loving attention to his unborn baby he can be certain that the baby is in turn responding.

"The parents must have found out that their baby is a boy. The father feels happy but also guilty. He is not supposed to like boys. This baby has lit up a previously activated pattern with males. His wife's sense of dread is now more conscious. She feels she will somehow lose this baby to her husband; that they will have something together that she will never be able to have. She has a desperate longing that she feels will never be fulfilled."

Having a baby should be a selfless endeavor. Because of that fact, the experience will "*light up*" and put you up against your deepest fears, patterns, and weak points.

You are becoming the sum-total of your every choice. You began this human process, probably, when you were conceived, but your choices didn't become scientifically noticeable until you became a fetus.

"The unborn baby is copying her mother who is subconsciously angry with her husband on a continual basis. The baby is afraid of her mother's anger and because of this will not express anger to her. But, she will express anger to her father because he is passive and she is not afraid of him. The baby's anger toward her father is in reaction to his desire to own her and be special to her. She would like that attention, but is afraid of her mother's control. The baby has reached out to her father many times before, and her mother had put a cloud of gray energy on her when she did.

So, out of fear, she is now siding with her mother."

As incredible as these scenarios may seem, these subconscious and psychic interactions are the manifestations of enacting either a basically fearful or a basically angry disposition. The selfish choices are coming out of the disposition. Our behavior patterns always spring from our core basic selfish disposition—angry or fearful. We can usually recognize the conscious or top side of these involvements in our families, we just don't usually see the hurtful energetic underneath part.

Your character is a manifestation of your spirit, your soul, your deepest intention for or against what is right, true, loving, and lovingly responsible. You have the tools. Now you have to consistently use them if you want to build a character that will sustain you in right and loving ways throughout your life.

Looking back, your most basic choice was a choice for either anger or fear. That means you somehow decided to approach life from either an angry stance or a fearful one. Your choice for one or the other is now your basic mode of behavior when you are choosing to act selfishly. You have shown this behavior by your actions in the womb that are observable by sonogram.

"The father is jealous of his wife's (imagined) relationship with the baby. He has gold ownership energy on his daughter. The fetus feels his energy as an assault on her, which it is. She is taking in what is

happening with her parents, as well as the sounds in her environment, but she is not reaching out as she should be by now. This is showing a basically fearful reaction."

The choice to approach life's circumstances from a place of anger or fear is a selfish choice. It is made so early (about two-and-a-half to three months in the womb) that it is considered innate. However, since you essentially have full awareness of what is right and the ability to choose for it, you are not innately selfish. You can choose against selfishness anytime you are willing. You can observe yourself doing this and you will agree that this is true. You will see that when you negatively react to your life's situations, you will typically use the specific mode of behavior that you have chosen.

After that first choice for anger or fear, you immediately went on to make another important selfish choice that will cause you much conflict from here on out. You went into negative agreement with one parent, the parent of similar angry or fearful disposition as your own.

Negative agreements with her father: "The agreements have to do with mental or intellectual attitudes: to be like him and to be sensitive. Also, to live in her mind the way he lives in his mind. This agreement is like a bonding sense or a sense that the fetus will be as the father wants her to be."

Because they are selfish, agreements become complicated. This unborn baby girl is in agreement with her father. She will probably often defy him because she will come to feel she is being controlled by him. Nonetheless, the basic agreements will still stand unless she identifies them, understands them, and changes them.

Although you are drawn to your parent with the same basic disposition, this dynamic is not true for adults. Most adults in a long-term marriage or relationship will be attracted to a partner of opposite disposition. So, you have one parent who is basically angry and one who is basically fearful. According to the basic disposition you have chosen, you were attracted to your parent of similar disposition.

"More than anyone, her two-year-old son knows how to get her angry by the things he does. She tells herself he doesn't mean it and he is just learning; but I am seeing he regularly defies and provokes her on purpose. She screams at him and her fetus seems to be aware of their interactions. The unborn baby ventures out and communicates energetically with her brother and feels they have a bond together. This is another reason why the mother gets agitated. Subconsciously she knows this and feels that they are siding against her."

Her husband, son, and daughter (in the womb) all have a similar fearful disposition. This creates a subconscious energetic alliance among them. Their basically angry mother approaches life from a place of anger rather than fear. Her energetic feel is totally different, so in a very real way she feels estranged from her family. Of course, consciously she has no idea why she feels the way she does.

It has been a while now that you have been living with your selfish choices. You have developed a lot during this time and have become increasingly aware of your womb space and outside energies impacting on you. Sadly, if you are like most of us, you are negatively reacting to the hurtful choices of both your parents. Thankfully, you are also responding to your parents' genuine caring with a choice to be peaceful and content.

"This baby is feeling a sense of emotional security and contentment. His mother's genuine caring and feelings of affection are consoling him."

You are having mental and emotional experiences that are posing quite a challenge. You are learning about your body and how to use it. You are having new discoveries at every turn. On top of all that, you are coming up against an entirely new dimension to your psychological existence. Almost to your dismay and disbelief, you are experiencing painful energies from the outside that you have no control over. You need to deal with this. It is scary and confusing. However, you do have the tools, and you innately know what they are and how to use them.

It takes courage and character to do what you innately know you should do in such situations. When you choose to respond without reacting negatively to hurtful energies coming at you, you will have an amazing discovery. You will realize (a "*eureka*" moment) that you can live in the rightness of your world (physical body and discovery) and experience contentment rather than mental, emotional, and physical pain.

"The twins are playing with each other, showing affection, and being in their own world together. They can sense the energy of the other and determine things about each other. They have been doing this since they were tiny embryos. This experience and ability seem to be physical as well as psychic. Many twins feel love for each other and a sense of companionship that is beyond words."

When you focus on your physical growth, and on discovering your ever-new abilities and the space in which you live, this will be your involvement and experience rather than the negative one. This happens because you are focusing on what you should be doing rather than getting caught up in negative reactions. This may not seem true in an immediate frightening or painful happening, but your right and loving responses to painful and scary energies will help you in ways you could not have foreseen. There is much good to be experienced that you will miss out on when you become involved in negative reaction.

"The baby is experiencing a sense of aliveness; this is helping him to move and explore. He is also feeling a sense of physical security and contentment related to his choices to explore and feel the health of his physical body. This activity is enhancing his emotional life."

"This fetus is withdrawing to an extreme. His mother is angry at what she has to go through to have this baby. She is also restricting and controlling her unborn baby with hurtful energy. If this fetus continues to stay within and not venture out because of his fear he will have an extremely distorted view of his experience. He will not learn the many things he should. These kinds of choices may cause serious effects after birth. The child may be very inward or self-absorbed or in the extreme may display symptoms of an autistic child."

Choices for anger in the womb also have ramifications that can be ongoing for a lifetime. If a fetus continually strikes out in anger, that pattern of reaction may lead to aggressive types of behavior, or a personality with symptoms of depression or, simply, a disgruntled child.

To the extent that you make right choices your life will be secure and inwardly content. More than that, by not reacting you will be able to see the truth of the situation to which you are responding. Even though you are only a fetus you will get to see the larger picture!

Unborn babies responding to their parents' hurtful choices:

"The struggle of a five-month-old fetus: She is at the effect of the battles her parents are having. There are times when she is keeping herself occupied by exploring her body and womb space. These are choices that make her feel good. But many times, she feels overpowered by her reactions to the hurtful energies she experiences and goes inward. Then she comes out again and focuses on her body's movements and has a good feeling.

However, she is ignoring many of the harsh energies inundating her. Mentally running from negative energies is making her stressed and not able to ascertain her actual situation. She is not learning as she should because she often does not follow her natural instincts to observe and learn as many fetuses do."

"This baby knows that when she focuses on the life of her body and its growth she feels content and secure."

Feeling the growth energy can be amazing. That feeling is an option for every fetus just for the choosing. But sadly, all too often unborn babies get caught up in feeling rejected and not loved and go inward—a choice that is a detriment to the baby's experience of life.

"Here at the fifth month the father has his attention on the baby saying, 'You are special to me.' He didn't care about the baby until he learned that the baby was a boy. The fetus is not reciprocating. I'm just seeing messages going in. The baby is guarding himself against the controlling energy in the father's message; so, he is refusing this communication. The fetus is feeling the father's possessive energy but doesn't know what it means. He only knows that he is threatened by it."

The baby is rejecting his father's communication by not responding. I think this is good, but it is not enough to help him be secure. I have seen fetuses forming loving bonds with siblings when they are being treated badly by their parents, going where the love is, and experiencing that instead of hurtful energies!

"This fetus is strongly picking up on his mother's feelings of uncertainty and anger. He hears her voice, but recoils because of her hurtful, emotional energies. The baby is moving around and kicking, but he remains frozen in fear. He does have some relaxing moments, but not many. The subconscious negative exchanges between his parents are extremely destructive. He is afraid to look out. He does not want to read his parents' thoughts and feelings."

This baby is going into a state of avoidance. He does not want to see what is there to see. This is becoming a behavior pattern that he will most likely bring forward into his life. He is not learning as he should be. He looks out sometimes, but he should be almost constantly exploring. This choice will also reflect later in his childhood. If this pattern continues he will not be able to understand as he should, he will be a slow learner and, generally, will not be interested in life.

How parents create hurtful energies that are felt by their babies:

"The fetus has gone into basic negative agreement with his father. The fetus has an energetic thrust toward his father. That is, with no thoughts or feelings, just an energetic attraction and tie. The father is basically angry; as is the fetus. The fetus is being covered with the mother's angry energy. She is totally beside herself because, subconsciously, she knows her baby has gone into agreement with her husband. She is irate and feels left out.

The baby and his father have a relationship, and she is on the outside. She just cannot stand this; her reaction is extremely irrational. She thinks her strong feelings are about her suspicion that her husband is being unfaithful. However, this is not the case; her extreme feelings are being triggered by old patterns of competition being activated regarding her parents and siblings."

Every selfish choice, no matter what the reason or how old you are, has negative consequences. These consequences are obvious in every single excerpt about parents and babies.

"There is red abrasive energy on this fetus. The father is jealous. He feels and believes that his wife has a special connection with his baby that he doesn't have. His angry, jealous energy is being projected at his wife and onto the baby inside of her. I think a man might know about the emotions I'm describing, but he would not be conscious that he was hurting his baby."

Honesty, honesty, honesty! I firmly believe that all negative situations in relationships can be solved and healed with sincere honest admitting of thoughts and feelings; although expression absolutely must be accompanied by a caring and loving attitude. So many painful experiences and situations could be alleviated and healed if only we would have the courage to lose whatever it is that we don't want to lose that keeps us being dishonest and closed.

"For this mother, the time is going slow. She wants it to be over. She is telling herself she will never do this again. She complains in this way to her boyfriend, but does not mean a lot of what she says. Sometimes the life inside of her feels good. The energy causing the baby's physical growth is extremely positive and gives her a certain sense of well-being that she ordinarily

does not have. She does not feel it when she is choosing to be negative. This mother does have quite a bit of instability and her baby feels the highs and lows her mother is experiencing."

When someone gets very selfish and starts acting like a brat, we may call him or her childish or say that person just never grew up. But, I think we all know some children who have never behaved as selfishly as the people we find ourselves calling *"childish"* because of their extreme selfish behavior.

At six months, you are preparing for birth into the physical world both psychologically and physically. Medical science tells us that you are already developing a unique personality. The sixth month is a period of rapid growth for you. Your weight will almost double. By the end of the month you will be 14 inches long and your feet 2 inches long. Your footprints and fingerprints are continuing to form; and you will weigh about 1.6 pounds. Your taste buds have fully developed and you are starting to fill the space in your mother's womb.

"The baby is growing fast. His movement and his attention-out are making him extremely aware. He knows his father does not want him. He knows his mother can cause him physical discomfort. He is aware that he has a sister. He knows when his mother is moving around and when she is sitting still. He knows when she is sleeping. Usually a pressure comes off him

at that time because she is physically relaxed, which relieves her stress and his. Also, she is subconsciously processing her deepest feelings through dreams, so she is not actively bombarding him with her thoughts in relation to him and the pregnancy.

This is a good time for the fetus; he relaxes and sleeps. He knows this time is free of the pressures of smoking and drinking. It is a clear time for him. This is when he recuperates. He has tried to tune-in to his father at these times but his father is not interested."

Your brain is developing rapidly. As your brain growth continues, you have brainwave activity for the visual and auditory systems starting to develop. You have patterns of sleep and activity which your mother will come to know. In addition, your lungs are forming branches of the respiratory tree as well as cells that produce surfactant. This substance will help your air sacs inflate once you reach the outside world.

"At six months: Joan will touch Jan and try to console her when she withdraws. Joan will try to get Jan to come out by touching her, and if she doesn't come out she'll kick her or bite her. Joan wants Jan to touch her."

Your skin is wrinkled and red. It is covered with fine soft hair and an oily substance. Real hair and toenails are beginning to grow. Fatty sheaths which transmit electrical impulses along nerves are forming. Your bones are becoming solid. You are starting to make breathing movements, but there is no air in your lungs yet. Your eyes are beginning to open. If you are a girl, you are developing eggs in your ovaries.

"The mother feels energetic and good. The red energy I'm seeing is indicating her physical health and well-being. She has a feeling of vitality because she is so physically fit and active. The red energy feels good to the fetus. It is creating an exciting feeling."

It is becoming obvious to me while looking at fetuses that the sense of well-being that accompanies a mother's physically fit body is a great help to the baby both physically and emotionally.

A fetal brain scan shows that you can respond to touch. Your parents' touching and playing with you is now possible, and you can respond through your mother's belly wall. Your muscle coordination is such that you can put your thumb in your mouth. Sucking your thumb calms you and strengthens your cheek and jaw muscles. You have become very active.

As you can see, you have a lot to put your attention on; there is a lot to keep you busy. You really don't need to be reacting. At every turn, you are making many interesting discoveries, you have growth to experience and new abilities to try out. You should be much too busy to be reacting to your parents' negativity. Maybe someday you will learn this, choose this, and your world will be dramatically different.

"This fetus seems to be preparing himself for his birth into the physical world not only physically, but, also, psychologically. He can see and sense energies. He is seeing different colors and ascertaining their meaning according to their color and feel. He is seeing thoughts as pictures and understands their meaning. He can distinguish between positive and negative energies by color and feel. He is acutely aware of his surroundings outside of the womb. He hears the voices that are close by and has come to know each person by his or her sound, energy, and feel. He also senses and knows how each one in his family thinks and feels about him at any given moment. Observing this fetus, he has been very outgoing and active since his fourth month. Now at six months, involvement with his family is something that happens on a regular basis throughout the day."

Here, at six months in the womb, I would like to take a break from our fetus baby. In the next chapter, I will be talking about character and personality, how they differ, and how we create a pseudo personality.

Four
Character and Personality

"Your every intention, choice, thought, feeling, action, and reaction creates your attitude and shapes your character and personality in either positive or negative ways."

Your character comprises the sum-total of your every right and wrong, loving and selfish intention and choice. It is also who you are in the moment with a right or a wrong choice. Over time your character will demonstrate your essence. With consistent choices, one way or the other, you build a character that is you. This is true because you have built your choices firmly into your conscious and subconscious mind, and you exercise your will to repeat the same kinds of choices again and again.

Your character is the result of your conscious and subconscious choices relating to your intentions, good or bad (loving or selfish). You can pretend you have good intentions when you do not; you can create a positive personality when you are not actually being positive. But, that will never change how you are in reality. You cannot change the truth about yourself unless you change your wrong, unloving choices and intentions. In that way, you are changing your character.

Every intention, choice, thought, feeling, action, and reaction creates your attitude and shapes your character and personality in either positive or negative ways. Positive, healthy personalities are the result of ongoing right, loving, truthful, and lovingly responsible choices. Dysfunctional personalities develop over time with many consistent, severely wrong choices. Your character becomes what people expect from you because of your previous unswerving choices one way or the other. I think we can all agree that a person's character is the result of his or her basic consistent ongoing choices for right and loving, or for wrong and selfish intentions and actions.

I'd like to go back to the beginning. As stated earlier, we begin making choices to form our characters early in the womb. According to medical tests the first observable sign of an unborn baby making choices is at about three months. It was shown that fetuses will either get angry or be fearful when they are faced with unwanted changes in their environments.

That means that, by that early age, we have already made a choice to approach life's circumstances from a basically angry or basically fearful mode of behavior.

This choice is not a mental choice; it is an expression of your will as a being, a Human Being. This choice becomes the base and the essence of your selfish character. Your innate ability to know and choose for right choices is the base and essence of your natural, innate character.

Human Beings are pure potential; we always choose one way or the other. It is often said that there are many roads to the top of the mountain. That, sadly, is the selfish mountain. There are only two roads that we choose from. Only one road will lead us to a better life, and it is always our choice one way or the other. We are constantly at small, but important, fork-in-the-road decisions. We can and often do get very lost when we choose the wrong fork in the road.

I think a choice for selfishness has been made so early, and is so basic that, that is the reason we find ourselves having to constantly choose against it (our selfish inclinations) if we want to feel good and feel good about ourselves. We all experience this inner conflict that sometimes becomes a battle. I'm sure most of us have often asked ourselves why we have this battle between what we want and what we know is right.

Why is it set up that we need to keep going against ourselves to do what we know is right? Why were we made this way? Doesn't it seem cruel? We blame God for so much of our "nature." But, it is really our basic choice for selfishness that is to blame. It is our essential choice for selfishness that makes it so difficult for us to consciously go against our selfish inclinations; even though when we do, it always feels good and sometimes better than good.

This is such an ingrained problem within us that we end up making choices that we know are wrong and then make them "right" in our minds. Then we go on to create elaborate excuses for our wrong choices that we insist are "right." Many of us blame this dilemma on being innately flawed, which we <u>definitely</u> are not. All these dynamics tie in together to create one big mess. It's like I keep saying the same things over and over from different angles. That is because <u>we</u> have created all the angles.

Nonetheless, understanding helps greatly in unlocking the door to facing the truth about ourselves. It also helps us to act in unselfish ways without having that inner conflict. Understanding why we do the negative things we do makes it easier to sincerely acknowledge when a choice is right and choose for it. When we do this our selfish desire seems to be left behind. In many instances, it has become nonexistent. It is not a focus; rightness becomes our focus and the battle has become a momentary thing, rather than the other way around.

Every selfish choice we make is acted out as an extension of that first choice to be basically angry or basically fearful. Our next most important selfish choice involves energetically siding with our parent of similar disposition; angry or fearful. Remember, with adults, opposites attract so typically you will have one basically angry parent and one basically fearful. When you have made this choice, you have agreed (in a bonding sense) to many modes of behavior, typically to be as that parent is or wants you to be.

This basic choice is especially significant. When you agree to be as a parent wants you to be, you seem to be relinquishing your free choice. But in fact, you are using your free choice to interact in a selfish way. You have a selfish reason for your choice. Again, this pertains to you the being, the Human Being, using your innate will not your brain.

Keep in mind, at every moment we are making choices. Right here, as a three-month-old fetus, you are making choices that not only determine the quality of your life experience in the womb but for many years to come. The more selfish agreements and choices you make the more entangled and complicated your life will be. When we choose to act on our parental agreements consistently they become patterns of behavior within our consciousnesses. These are visible after birth. Choosing to enact agreements is why some of us are more like one parent and some more like the other parent. This is also a complicated dynamic that when played out often becomes perplexing. Acting out parental agreements adds a level of confusion as to who we are and a level of stress that we did not have to endure.

In some important ways, your personality is different from your character. We can manipulate our personalities in many ways. We can't do that with our characters. Our characters are who we are in truth. They are the sum-total of the good and bad of us. Our personalities are also the sum-total of the good and bad of us. However, the difference is that we can create what I would call a pseudo-positive personality. That is, we can appear to be positive, when, in fact, we are not. This could be over a lifetime or simply in a certain moment.

A pseudo-positive personality is an image that we create and project to others; it is usually acknowledged as who we are. However, your character is who you truly are, not the image you tell yourself, pretend to be, and project to others.

We may be able to hide our negative aspects with conscious positive appearances but over time, or in stressful situations, that negative truth will manifest in a certain kind of hurtful behavior or dysfunction. Typically, once set, personalities and personality disorders tend to be stable, longlasting, persist, and worsen across a person's lifespan. This is true only because most of us refuse to admit to the true causes of our negative behaviors. In not acknowledging the cause we have no way of dealing with a problem behavior.

Changing your character for good does not include pretense. You can pretend to have good intentions when they are not; you can create a positive personality when you are not actually being positive. Pretending to be good does not make us good. It makes us less good and more complicated.

You can't build a truly positive personality on top ofself-seeking hidden intentions. When you do that you are just piling on the negativity. You cannot change the truth about yourself unless you change your basic wrong intentions and choices. In that way, you are changing your character. You are also changing your personality for the better. To the extent that we create personalities from ideas, beliefs, agreements, and behavior patterns we will create illusion, and also create more than one personality. Typically, most of us display a public personality and a private personality, so to speak. Some people have created many variations of a personality because they think it is a more efficient way to interface with a variety of people or circumstances. When we do this to an extreme, however, we become "mentally ill." It is funny how we can view some kinds of behavior as okay in moderation but in the extreme they become "mental illnesses."

Sadly, creating a personality with a selfish intention is something all of us do. This is where you can make right seem wrong and wrong seem right. Here is where you can manipulate the truth in any way you want and believe it. Here is where we have become dangerously complicated. You can manipulate your personality with choices to be this way and that; you can change your personality with choices to think and feel different ways to accomplish desired goals. We always manipulate our personalities for selfish reasons to get what we want or to avoid what we don't want in one situation or another.

When a person's true colors come out, it means that he or she (in that moment) is seen in truth. The person's self-created personality is stripped away (probably by a certain action) and his or her core intention becomes visible. I talked earlier about the split of having an opposite conscious and subconscious or hidden intention. As I explained before, when a person has a right and loving conscious and subconscious intention, what you see is what you get! True colors are out there for all to see. It is usually only our wrong intentions that we try to hide.

How do we, in fact, create a pseudo-positive personality? We usually create pseudo-positive personalities without consciously realizing what we are doing. When we act on selfish desires we create a pseudo-positive personality and set it into motion.

What we want determines a lot of who we are. We build our pseudo-positive personalities with certain ideas and beliefs and with agreements with our parents and others. We especially build our pseudo-positive personalities by building and using our behavior patterns and all of their associated ideas, beliefs, and feelings.

What is the process? Pseudo-positive thoughts and feelings are the tools that a person uses to turn on and sustain a reality (illusion) and experience by enacting pre-recorded behavior patterns. Pseudo-positive thoughts and feelings in a sense are not real. They usually have little to do with the truth of a person's internal or external realities and circumstances.

Pseudo-positive thoughts and feelings are created by consciously thinking thoughts repeatedly and storing them in your subconscious bank of ideas. This practice is a common conscious technique for improving your mental and emotional stance and experience. This technique is used in some meditation practices. The idea is that the more energy you consciously put into certain ideas by thinking about them, the easier and quicker you will be able to have an emotional experience of euphoria or joy, or any other desired feeling that the repeated thoughts are meant to produce.

As far as meditation is concerned, you can quiet your mind but there is never a time when you are not intending, choosing, thinking, and feeling. A meditation activity is a matter of _what_ you are intending and choosing, not _if._ I am not qualified to speak of all meditation, but I think it is safe to say that much of the spiritual experience involved in many types of meditation is brought about by focusing on repeated thoughts to attain certain feelings. This is exactly what <u>we</u> do (mostly without knowing it) to create a behavior pattern and have it ready to put into use.

Another common technique in consciously using pseudo-positive thoughts and feelings is to create a desired positive personality. The _"Power of Positive Thinking"_ and _"How to Win Friends and Influence People"_ are a couple of old-time popular methods that use this process. I'm sure there must be many new programs with the same old ideas and techniques. In this technique, you are creating and sustaining a programmed experience with much conscious and subconscious intention, thought, desire, and effort. You are living solidly in behavior patterns when you make this technique a major part of your life.

I think the reason this method of changing your ideas to change yourself became popular (and I suspect still is) is that it is easy to change your ideas (when you want to), but not so easy to change your basically selfish intentions. So, in a way, you get a quick fix without in fact changing your inner self, the self that is insecure and hurting because of your self-serving intentions and choices. Of course, when you are in this mode, you need to constantly work to sustain a way of being that is almost impossible to sustain on an ongoing basis. Nonetheless, amazingly some people do, and suffer from being enormously unreal.

Another common use for pseudo-positive thoughts and feelings is one that is not consciously orchestrated. It is a conscious choice to trigger and enact a subconscious behavior pattern. This is when a person suddenly, at first glance, "falls in love" with another. All those thoughts and feelings come out of a pre-programmed wishful subconscious behavior pattern and most often have nothing to do with the person being admired.

Pseudo-positive behavior patterns can often be seen in people with serious dysfunctions and mental illnesses. For example, the manic side of a manic-depressive personality can often appear positive, but it is never actually positive. It is part of a destructive behavior pattern. It requires much subconscious and conscious effort to keep the "positive" behavior alive. It is unsustainable because the person is enacting a destructive pattern that includes the positive pretense.

According to the many clairvoyant readings I have done on Alzheimer's patients, the condition is a strong enactment of behavior patterns both pseudo-positive and negative. A schizophrenic personality enacts pseudo-positive thoughts and feelings that are obvious illusions. Every person with a serious dysfunction is steeped in acting out behavior patterns. He or she is consistently subconsciously activating pattern networks that involve many strong destructive and illusionary pattern ideas and feelings.

Our self-built positive personalities contribute greatly to our overall character. They put weight on the negative side. Yes, your positive ideas about yourself and your life that are not essentially true add negative substance to your character. Your character is, at all times, the sum-total of your choices, including your choices to pretend or to be positive when you are in fact not being positive. All of this complex orchestration is always driven by selfish and self-centered desires; desires to have or desires not to have. In other words, to get what we want in one way or another, or to avoid what we don't want.

What are behavior patterns? I think we all have felt driven at times to do something that was obviously wrong. That is when we somehow manage to convince ourselves that our destructive drives are alien, external, or beyond our control. But of course, we know that is not true. The culprit is subconscious behavior patterns that we consciously choose to act out.

Behavior patterns consist of ideas, opinions, and beliefs with their related feelings. They become patterns when we consistently repeat a set of ideas, opinions, and beliefs. Behavior patterns are permanently recorded within us.

We subconsciously know precisely where to go in our consciousnesses to turn on our patterns, to accelerate them, and to turn them off. We cannot erase or eliminate them. We can only choose not to act on them and not to energize the ideas and feelings involved. When we do the pattern will remain dormant. We can use patterns to keep ideas and feelings active for an entire lifetime. When we suppress an angry pattern, it may come into our conscious awareness as irritability, sarcasm, or just plain old crankiness. Suppressed fear may manifest consciously as anxiety, insecurity, nervousness, or excessive and unreasonable concern. Also, the strength of a drive (pattern) increases when we are trying to suppress it. The strength also increases when we are consciously avoiding and distancing from our true intentions.

When we act on a behavior pattern we fill it with energy. With enough determination and desire, we may ignite many or all of the ideas in the pattern. The ideas in the pattern are the excuses that we consistently give ourselves (and believe) for defending our actions. When we use these excuses often, they eventually become beliefs that we swear by to justify our behavior. Nonetheless, if we begin to activate a pattern we can minimize the charge by understanding the why of the pattern, and by having a willingness to stop. We can stop in midstream so to speak when we are willing.

We decide on the amount of commitment we will have to the ideas and feelings of a pattern. We regulate the degree of our conviction to keep the pattern going; and we choose when to end it. We do all of this with interrelated conscious and subconscious choices. We start and end our patterns always with a deliberate conscious and subconscious intention and choice.

We all have experienced that our thoughts create certain feelings in us. In addition, our memories contain thoughts and feelings. When we think a thought that is related to a behavior pattern we are triggering (on purpose) that subconscious pattern. Then, we usually have a rush of related thoughts and feelings that seem to be automatic. Another point is that sometimes our feelings can be so intense that they seem to be without thoughts. But thoughts always trigger feelings. You can't identify a pattern unless you investigate the thoughts that are instigating the feelings. It is easy to identify a behavior pattern when you become angry, afraid, arrogant, insecure, or any number of behaviors that feel overwhelming and are obviously hurtful. But you can also learn to recognize patterns in your day-today living that are less severe.

Believing is an important factor in acting out a behavior pattern. To the extent that we consciously believe the validity or necessity of thinking and feeling a certain way, we will react from a chosen behavior pattern's ideas and feelings. Because of our strong desires and beliefs on certain issues, we end up repeating those ideas and feelings again and again; making them stronger with each choice. They eventually become what we see as being automatic. This is because when our desire is strong just one thought or one feeling can trigger all the thoughts and feelings in a behavior pattern.

Our more complicated and puzzling behaviors are often comprised of several interconnected patterns. This network of patterns when consciously or subconsciously triggered can feel overwhelming. An active network of patterns can be obvious when the patterns relate to selfserving drives that may seem to be beyond our control like eating, drugs, or alcohol. Or, on the psychological side, jealousy, envy, anger, fear, and a myriad of other feelings that we tell ourselves we cannot stop.

There are also some not so obvious pattern networks that we activate during the routines of our everyday lives. These can sometimes be more dangerous because we take them for granted as true or not so important. We don't think there is anything wrong with our thoughts and feelings so we don't even try to change them. An example: You are holding in your consciousness (conscious and subconscious) a group of ideas and feelings about your partner and child.

This is a pattern network that you have developed from experience over some years. You have ideas and feelings about how they are, or how they interact, what is right about them and what is wrong about them.

Remember, firm belief is necessary to sustain a pattern in your consciousness. You believe you are right, so much so that you take your thoughts and feelings for granted. The danger of an attitude and pattern like this one is that you are not in a mental position to see your partner and child as they are in truth. This is a good example of having an attitude of being right when you are not actually right. You are not right because you are in your ideas of what you think is right and accurate. If you want to see the truth you have to be willing to be wrong and put your ideas on suspension. That will put you in a mental and emotional position to see what is true.

An example: You may be thinking something about your child that was true before and probably will be true again. But, at that moment, your child may be off somewhere and he or she is intending and choosing to be very different than the way you are thinking about him or her at the time.

If you practice, to get out of that certain pattern of thinking, really get out of it, you would be able to know your child's intention and choice in that moment even when he or she is miles away. You can do this because you are in another zone, so to speak.

You are "outside the box," outside of your patterns. You become able to see and know the truth in the moment. Another important point is that when you are not enacting a pattern you give those around you the space to change or to be themselves without the burden of your opinions. Even when you are not being verbal about your thoughts and feelings they are felt and are obvious to those around you.

We are literally human telepathic machines. We may not consciously know what others are thinking and feeling, but we always know subconsciously. More than that, we act and react consciously to what we are sensing and seeing in others on that subconscious level. With enough willingness, you will be able to bring much of the content of your subconscious mind to your conscious awareness, as well as the life you experience on that subconscious level. When you are willing to become aware of a pattern that you enact, it becomes possible to work to change that pattern. In doing this you will go beyond your ideas and feelings. You will choose to step outside of your pattern. This experience is like being in another universe. We all like the idea of being free. Stepping out of our patterns can make us free in a way that we rarely experience.

When enacting a mental and emotional pattern it is impossible to see the actual truth about oneself, or about another person or a situation. I would venture to say that when someone gets a truly wonderful inspiration for something new, never thought of before, that person is totally outside of the box of his or her behavior patterns. With enough observation and practice, you will be able to identify the nature of a pattern and where it might have originated. When you begin to understand your patterns and why you enact them, you will most likely have a desire and a willingness to change them. This kind of change is entirely different than trying to force yourself to stop a pattern (drive) by using willpower. Understanding the truth of why we have selfish intentions and drives is like a great big door to willingness. But it is not until we go through that door consistently that we will experience this truth.

Your behavior patterns play a major role in shaping your pseudo-positive personality. We enact our pseudopositive personalities when we are acting out one of our many behavior patterns. When we routinely repeat a certain behavior to attain a goal, I think we can all recognize that we are enacting a pattern.

As I explained before, patterns are programmed reactions and responses. When enacted they can appear to be negative or appear to be positive. We use patterns when we are in negative reaction to a person or situation. We also use patterns when we are striving to obtain an extremely desired person or objective. Much of the time, an ego is built by consistently acting out pattern ideas and feelings to attain certain goals regarding the way we want to see ourselves, and what we want to be or become. However, when we are truly acting rightly, those right choices create a positive ego which gives us a true and secure sense of self-esteem.

When enacting behavior patterns our behavior will range from minimal to extreme according to our conscious and subconscious plan. We usually know that we can manage or stop our minimal reactions; but, we may feel it is impossible to stop or to change our stronger ones. This is never true because we are in full control at all times. We are consciously and subconsciously triggering the specific behavior patterns we want to use. We also decide just how much energy to put into them to accomplish our goals.

We also know where the switch is to turn off our pattern ideas and feelings. We simply have to be willing to do it. Here is an example of this ability. Have you ever been in so much negative reaction to someone that you felt you were almost losing it? Then, in that moment, something important happened—perhaps an accident or a similar urgency. In an instant, you suddenly became a different person. The reaction was gone and you were dealing with the serious mishap. You stopped on a dime.

Since we are conducting the entire process we are never helpless to stop our drives and negative behaviors. You knew exactly how to do it, and you did it. This kind of action shows that we have the full ability to stop any behavior at any time; we just have to be willing.

When you are enacting a pseudo-positive pattern it often means that you are acting positively for an underlying selfish or wrong reason. I would like to talk more about the patterns that we take for granted and live with every day. Understanding, identifying, and working to change patterns that are not so severe can help us prepare to tackle our stronger ones. We can practice on the not so difficult patterns and sneak up on those we find impossible to change.

As I said, the biggest obstacle to changing our seemingly not so negative pattern behaviors is that we think they are okay and not hurting anyone. This is a convenient misconception. We think this way because we hold many beliefs and attitudes that support the positive appearance of a selfish intention and action. We see them as being truly positive.

A common mistake that causes us inner trouble is that we do the right thing for the wrong reason, essentially a self-serving reason. That causes conflict within us rather than contentment. Another obstacle to recognizing a self-seeking pattern is when we want something (or someone) that in our view may appear to be good or good for us. Remember, we are thinking the thoughts and feeling the feelings of a specific pattern of wanting something. In light of that, we are not seeing clearly. It does not mean that the person or thing is not right for us, but we won't have a sense of certainty or clarity until we come from a truly loving place in that instance.

So, we act on the thoughts and feelings we have created in the pattern and, as always, sooner or later it turns into a negative experience. When this happens we almost always put the blame onto something other than the actual cause, which is the initial enactment of a selfish pattern and playing out the ideas and feelings involved therein. I think all too many of us can relate to this scenario in regard to our relationships as well as many other types of involvements. When we want something badly enough it is easy to view selfish patterns and maneuvers as being positive or having a positive benefit. Yet, I don't think any of us have found this to be the case.

For a better understanding of what a pattern might look like, here are a few examples. A significant common pattern involves variations and degrees of being absent minded. This pattern can be minimal or it can extend all the way to serious mental illnesses. All serious mental illnesses include this pattern as well as countless others. You begin to create this type of pattern when you consistently mentally and emotionally run, hide, or avoid painful life situations and suppress their memories. This pattern begins in the womb. It is a reaction to parental abuse (of any sort) over the period of a child's lifetime at home. The pattern is well reinforced by the time the child leaves the house. Sadly, the pattern has already been strongly set and the adult child will continue to use it probably throughout a lifetime. Patterns may fluctuate over the years, but they most often become increasingly severe as life continues.

I have found that, in most cases, the subconscious determination to enact a pattern involves the severity of abuse and the level of the child's ongoing reaction to the abuse. The degree and amount of reaction create the severity of the enactment of the pattern.

The ideas and related feelings in a pattern of absentmindedness might look like this:

"I don't want to be here. I am afraid to be here. I don't like my life. I feel lost with no one to love me. It is too hard to stay here. I don't want to live anymore. I feel demoralized. I can never get what I want or need. It is dangerous to confront and easier to avoid and hide. It is easier to be mentally and emotionally absent than to feel rejected and in pain." Perhaps, after a lifetime of passing on the abuse, there may be this thought: *"My hidden secrets are my own and I will go to my grave with them."*

The thoughts and feelings of a pattern don't stand alone. When enacted they roll out all kinds of destructive and self-destructive interactions and scenarios. In the less serious enactment of this pattern you may see people who are being inward, self-conscious, and forgetful. There are many levels of behavior before you get to the extreme. However, as explained, the extreme of this pattern can be enormously dangerous and disconcerting. Consistent and strong choices to enact such a pattern can lead a person into all kinds of serious mental dysfunctions.

Lying seems to be a universal pattern to varying degrees. I think we all lie on occasion. I think we lie to ourselves often, most of the time not even realizing that we are lying. It is a rare person who does not, to some degree, have a pattern of lying. A pattern of lying is a fear-based pattern, meaning that our most important lies are usually because we are afraid of an outcome.

However, another common use for lying is to present ourselves a little (or a lot) differently than we truly are. We may do this when we feel insecure and are afraid people won't like us. Or, we may just want to appear to be better than others.

There are many types of lies that are serious, that is, lies that have the definite potential for harm. There are also lies that try to cover wrongdoing. There are probably as many reasons for lying as there are individuals.

Here are some reasons people gave for lying.

"If I don't lie people will know the truth about me, and I won't get what I want. I have to lie because it

is impossible to be honest in my situation. If I don't lie I will be hurt. It is dangerous to tell the truth. It is more comfortable to lie; the truth hurts people. I can control situations better when I lie."

The list goes on and on, but you get the idea. For most people, it took a lot of work, honesty, humility, and sweat to express about their lies—sometimes to even just recognize them. Too many times we are afraid to expose the truth. Often the truth doesn't seem like an acceptable option. Sometimes it is embarrassing. In general, people do not like the truth so we make up our own. In thinking about our own reasons for lying and the situations that might go with them, we can better understand "the why" and know "the when" of using our own lying patterns.

A word of caution here: To tell someone the truth it must be appropriate. It cannot be a dumping. It cannot be using the truth as a weapon, which is so easy to do when we're angry. We have to check ourselves carefully to make sure we are not in reaction. We have to be in a responsible, loving place. If we are telling the truth about ourselves we must not grovel, that is, don't do it to get something.

This is such a tricky involvement, so much complication and enactment of subtle patterns and desires that it may be difficult to tell the truth cleanly. Here is where knowing our basic intention is critical. I would just say practice telling the actual truth until you get good at it, then it will become cleaner and easier. There are certain situations in which lying is a truly right choice—that is, when it is a truly loving act, not coming from a selfseeking motive. It could be to protect someone from harm. In many of these cases it takes enormous courage to deny the truth, because at such times you may have to risk your own safety.

It is obvious that we are enacting an anger pattern when we use anger for negative reasons. The definitions for the word anger are all hurtful attitudes: *"annoyance, irritation, fury, rage, antagonism, re-*

sentment." What about aggression? If you are aggressively going after a goal; isn't that positive? The dictionary would disagree: *"violence, hostility, anger, attack, assault, etc."* Yet, we still believe that anger can be behind a positive action.

It is common to use anger and anger patterns to attain "positive" goals or results. This is one place that we are <u>absolutely</u> sure that our intentions are right, good, and productive. But, you guessed it! There is always a selfish, self-serving, that is, negative intention driving the use of anger in all activities. When we compete, there is always stress because we want to win. No matter what the competition, even when we say that we are competing against ourselves (as in running) there is stress to attain a goal. We want something. That wanting comes from a selfish intention. It causes stress because we are being a way that we are not supposed to be. In a very real sense, selfishness goes against our very nature. It is a way that we were not created for so we suffer the effects of every selfish choice we make.

The idea that wanting something truly good is so ingrained within us that it may be hard to see that this is not true. Our selfish desire for good puts us in a position that we are unable to experience a true sense of good, content, elation, happiness, etc. We are not *"in the zone"* because we are in our patterns; we are in the box with all our ideas and beliefs. It is out of the box that we experience the truth of who we are as Human Beings. Being in our patterns is one reason we seem to be constantly searching to find ourselves. It is also why we keep trying to attain what we think happiness is and all that goes with it.

How do we get to see the truth about this enormous out-of-the-box perspective? There must be millions of examples of people who are implementing their desires for good. What about those people? We can look at so many instances and want answers to this question. However, the only way to know this truth is from within yourself. Work to get to see your true intentions in everything you do. You won't find the answer outside.

Here are some negative and "positive" responses people gave for reacting in anger. *"I feel powerful when I get angry. I get my way. People respect me; they* *see my power. It helps me to accomplish something good. People get afraid and do what I want. Anger pushes me to be superior. It sometimes makes me a better person. I can defend myself when I get angry. You need anger to get by in this world. I can control a situation better when I'm angry. I know it is wrong to be angry, but I just can't help it. I keep trying to stop because I see how hurtful it is; but I don't know how to stop. I just keep being angry until it is all out of me. I think that is a positive approach."*

Again, it takes much introspection to come up with these kinds of answers. We are so conditioned to believe our pattern's lies. It takes a certain amount of courage and willingness to be wrong about things we were convinced we were right about. It takes courage and willingness to see and acknowledge that we have been wrong over and over again. That is, for as many years as we have been enacting the pattern. That, for all of us, is before we can remember.

An obvious disadvantage to using behavior patterns is that, in that moment, we are not real. Sadly, that moment for many of us becomes a daily moment-to-moment experience that extends for an entire lifetime. Another drawback to enacting pattern ideas and their related feelings is that, at those times, we are not mentally and emotionally present to what is happening. We are instead present to our ideas, and usually our attention is on ourselves not the other person or the situation.

This fact about our attention and focus can be a clue to show us that we are enacting a pattern. If your focus is on yourself when you are interacting with a person or situation you are not present to that person or situation. That is why so many of us do not remember a person's name on our first meeting. We barely heard their name to begin with because our attention was firmly fixed on ourselves. When enacting a pattern, we are not acting from our innate sense of how we know we should be in that moment. Consequently, we don't get to experience the situation as it is in truth. We miss out on a lot when we enact our behavior patterns.

We all develop our characters in ways that we are not even consciously aware of, yet that doesn't matter. We don't need to consciously know everything about ourselves to have a character that comprises goodness, love, honesty, rightness, caring, giving, generosity, patience, that is, perseverance in good no matter what is coming at us. We can all do this. When we practice these obvious attributes, the rest will follow. The more truly right choices, the more we will understand and know our subconscious selves and all that goes with that understanding.

I will be talking about the process of change on an essential level in more depth. But, for right now, here are some ways you can shape your character and personality.

When you strive in each new moment to do what you feel, sense, and ultimately know is the right thing to do, you will be creating a unique character and personality. I say unique because you will be following an innate sense that is guiding you, rather than using selfish behavior patterns and creating a persona. Another reason you and your personality will be unique is that you won't know how you will be until the circumstance of the next moment presents itself. The more right choices you make, the more you will understand this concept and the less complicated you will become to yourself.

I don't mean to be a downer but there is something very real and important that I would like to point out. Going against your selfish inclinations and stepping out of the box of your ideas and beliefs is possibly the most difficult consistent choice you can make. This is hard stuff. It is not only hard, it is complicated. There seems to be a current popular craze. People are striving to excel in all kinds of new and old sports and endeavors. The young risk their lives and limbs as Ninja Warriors, etc. The not-so-young have their own challenges and put much courage and effort into accomplishing certain goals, physical and otherwise.

However, changing yourself on an essential level is an entirely different ballgame. To go against your deepseated selfish inclinations, to get out of the very ideas that you feel are helping you, or to leave behind the destructive drives that are so ingrained and familiar; who wants to do that? Who wants to believe that all of this is true? Who wants to believe that it is even possible to achieve? Is selfishness all that bad, all the time? Well, you know my answer; nonetheless, you must decide that answer for yourself. Now, let's get back to that precious little baby at seven months in the womb.

Five
Entering the Final Stages

"It is up to you to focus on rightness and love. These should be your 'North Star' now and for the rest of your life."

From the moment you were conceived, you were a Human Being with awareness and choice. You began to live within a minute human embryo body. To the extent that it was possible you manifested through that tiny body. As you grew you became increasingly aware of your embryo body as you were making choices that were necessary for you to grow, develop, and live. It is only when you reached your third month in your mother's womb that your choices became visible to scientific testing. But, of course, as <u>you</u> know, you have had a lifetime of choices and experiences so far! From this point onward, you will be increasingly more visible.

From the third through the sixth month you have had many learning experiences and have made countless choices about your ever-changing circumstances and interactions. The more you are developing, the more ability you have to express yourself through your tiny, but intrinsic and ever-growing physical body.

You are now entering into the final stages of your life in the womb. You will have the next three months to prepare to become a loving human baby. You have already decided that you will approach your life situations from a basically angry or a basically fearful position. You have already made choices relating to that original choice. You have already experienced that your right choices (and the right choices of your parents) have made your life so much easier.

So far, you have made right choices, and wrong choices and your parents have as well. It is up to you to focus on rightness and love. That should be your *"North Star"* now and for the rest of your life. You cannot depend upon the right choices of others for your security or contentment. You must depend upon your own. That is true now and you will find that it will be true always. As your life develops you will have many more opportunities to make right, honest, loving, and lovingly responsible choices. This is the most important and meaningful endeavor in which you will ever participate. Now, let's take a look at how your body and character are developing here at seven months in your mother's womb.

By now, at seven months in the womb, you are the size of a large butternut squash and are about 15 inches long. You weigh over 2 ½ pounds and are getting stronger by the minute. You are long enough that your mother feels your kicks; and they are much stronger. Your eyelids have been fused shut, but now you can open and close them at will. More than that, your irises are filled with pigment.

"For the most part, the father has psychically backed away. He subconsciously knows his daughter wants to connect with him but his wife punishes her with angry energy when she makes that attempt. The fact that his daughter wants to connect with him is enough for him. However, this subconscious knowledge about his wife's jealousy and control is the reason he feels he has given up about his wife and the baby."

"The baby's mother is excited. She is feeling that she is going to have her way. Consciously, she thinks she is excited because her baby is going to live. However, this mother is excited because her baby has communicated that she will belong to her to the exclusion of the baby's father. There is a definite image and feeling that says, 'I'll do whatever you want. I'll belong to you.'"

The fetus sees her mother's wishes as being linked to her well-being, instead of seeing that her right choices are the only things that will give her true security. This choice is setting into motion an extremely negative dynamic, which can appear to be positive. This agreement is becoming a form of bondage that can make a child appear to be *"good as* *gold.*" Her mother is relieved that her strong feelings of hatred, anger, and irritation have subsided. She still feels angry and irritated, but is putting the cause onto other issues. Most fetuses I have read do not go into such extreme negative agreement with a parent. But, usually go inward attempting to get away from a parent's control. This baby is allowing herself to be inundated by her mother's energetic expectations and demands.

"This fetus is in agreement with his father. His brother is in-agreement with his mother, so the brother is staying energetically clear of the unborn baby. There is a gray haze around the baby's head. He is afraid to look out. His mother has him traumatized, and he is afraid to be. Fear of looking out brings confusion and impedes his learning in relation to his body and his womb environment."

An ultrasound at seven months shows that your head is large in proportion to your body. Incredibly your brain accounts for 12 percent of your entire body weight and is developing rapidly. The part of your brain associated with intelligence and personality is becoming far more complex. You already have the 100 billion brain cells that you will have at birth. Nonetheless, connections still need to be made to form the neurological network that will give you control over everything from your speech to your footsteps.

"This mother is playing music and doing exercises that are making her fetus physically comfortable. Nonetheless, her mental possession of her baby is making him feel restricted. She has big plans for him that may seem harmless, but are not. When a mother's emotional state is consistently selfish and negative, it is often more hurtful to her fetus than what she may or may not be doing physically."

Anything a mother can do to help the comfort of her unborn baby is a good thing. Her mental and emotional choices and state are critical but negative thoughts and feelings are not always that easy to stop or change. When a mother sincerely wants her baby to be pain free and content she will find ways to do just that to the best of her ability.

"The baby is feeling a sense of physical security and contentment at this time, which is related to his mother's physical health. It is nourishing his physical and emotional condition."

"The baby is still moving around a lot. I'm seeing the father communicating to his son, and that is exciting the baby. He is responding by sending energy toward his father. He saw his father do this and he is copying him. These recent contacts are a relief for the fetus."

It is important that fathers know that they can communicate directly to their unborn babies. I say *"to"* because you probably will not sense a return communication. But, you should know that when you are communicating sincerely and unselfishly your baby will always respond to you. This kind of activity, when it is open and not hidden, may curtail any possessiveness (or a feeling of a special bond) on the part of the mother.

We have to remember that the baby is the special one in the situation. You are here to love and care for the baby. It is not the other way around. When you are truly (unselfishly) loving your baby, he or she will certainly be grateful for that and love you in return. Alas, this is another area where we often have our ideas and priorities upside-down and backwards. How do you know when you are loving your baby unselfishly? I would ask, "*Where is your attention and what are your desires?*" The answer to these questions will tell you where you stand.

While we're on this subject, "It is not about you." This is a statement that we should all glue to our eyeballs! This is a statement that we should say to ourselves every time we see ourselves thinking or choosing selfishly. When we are in a loving, unselfish mode it is never about us; it is always about what is right, honest, loving, and lovingly responsible.

"The baby's father is not willing to make a connection. This has pushed her toward her mother. She feels she has no choice. The baby did not come to this by thinking. It is more like seeing and intuiting the

truth of the situation and making choices concerning that truth. The sense I am getting from the baby is the feeling of, 'I can't go that way. He won't accept me.' She has the feeling of being swallowed up by her mother. She is afraid of that, but feels there is nowhere else to go."

Your lungs and digestive tract are almost fully developed. Your mother can get to know you by paying attention to how you react to different foods, sounds, and lights. You're not moving around as much because you are filling out your womb space. As you run out of room, you are bending your head toward your knees, curling as you did when you were tiny. You may already be getting ready for birth by turning upside-down. You instinctively know that your head should be pointing downward, ready for your journey into the world.

"The father still has controlling energy on the fetus, but it is not affecting her dramatically. This is because his attention is usually elsewhere so the impact of his energy is less intense. His energy is saying, 'I must be a part of your life.' However, he is thinking in the future, after she is born. This energy is somewhat controlling but it is not felt harshly; as is the mother's present time energy of negative thoughts and feelings."

"The fetus is physically active and emotionally upset. His mother is generally unhappy with her life.

She is dreading the constant care a newborn will require. She has two other children and feels this pregnancy is overwhelming. The fetus has a sense that his experience so far is all there is going to be."

By the seventh month, some fetuses I've read have made the connection that they will be on the outside at some point. This baby has a sense that this is all there will be. He keeps reaching out to his father and is relieved by his father's responses to him. The oldest brother is now also having pleasant exchanges with the baby.

It is important to remember that when reading these excerpts the reality and level that I am reading and describing is very different from our normal, everyday conscious level and reality.

The more a person is in touch with his or her subconscious (psychic) life and the more aware a person is of the subconscious reality in general, the more vulnerable that person will be to the positive and negative energies surrounding him or her. Since a fetus lives entirely on this subconscious (psychic) level, this is all he or she sees and feels. It is all a fetus relates to and experiences. What we see as a little negativity an unborn baby experiences as huge.

This is true because the greater part of our negativity is suppressed; that means that our negativity resides and is more real on that psychic, subconscious level of our existence. You can see the force of it when you let it into your conscious awareness, and even more when you express it verbally or physically. An unborn baby will always respond to the more real subconscious and psychic reality of parents; as well as any significant person in his or her environment.

There is something that I think I should mention here; it is about the psychic realm. There are different ways that you can learn to become aware of and experience the psychic realm. I would strongly advise against all of them.

There are psychics who can tell you things about yourself that you may think are fascinating. A psychic can tell you many things about yourself. But I guarantee, he or she will not tell you about your wrong choices, which most of the time are obvious to such a person. That is only because we live in a selfish world, and no one I know will pay money to hear bad things about themselves! Nonetheless, even when psychics are wellmeaning and accurate it may not be the right thing for you to do. Suppose a psychic tells you about a good event that will happen to you in the future. Guess who is going to be thinking about that event instead of getting on with your life, doing what is right and being loving?

Even the best psychics see only the potential future. They are following a psychological thread that they see or sense in you. That thread is the thread of your patterns, and other information that you have recorded in your consciousness which can be seen in your aura, i.e. your energy body. The psychic may be seeing your present time goals, dreams, aspirations, or fears which you have, yourself, projected into the future. Most psychics don't even understand how they do what they do or what they are, in fact, doing. Most often, they see the future as a certainty not a potentiality.

For all of us the future is written in pencil. As far as the future is concerned we can erase and rewrite it at any time. As I mentioned before, we cannot do that with our past. Our past is recorded permanently in our subconscious minds. We can de-energize our patterns and experiences but we cannot eliminate them.

Importantly, the psychic realm can be a scary place. It is real with real people playing out on a subconscious level. Many people who have wrong intentions are playing out their lives in negative roles on that level. This is obvious in the clairvoyant reading excerpts, although these excerpts are about people who are not horrifically negative. Also, there are disincarnate beings on that level that have refused to go on to where they are meant to be. They are there because they refuse to let go of what they insist on being attached to in the human realm. Some of the scary stories you may have heard, read about, or seen in movies are most often products of extremely creative imaginations, usually greatly enhanced. Nonetheless, they are modeled after a true reality.

Then there are those stories that are of actual real experiences of people interacting with that psychic realm. I believe that some of these happenings do exist but most are probably greatly exaggerated and misunderstood. Whatever the case, I firmly believe that it is best to stay away from all aspects of the psychic realm because it is not where we should be, and that, in itself, makes it dangerous.

The only safe way to enter into the psychic realm and to experience the reality I have been talking about is by going into your own subconscious to explore your deepest intentions, thoughts, feelings, and psychic actions. In that way, you are safe from all the weirdness, danger, and harm that can happen on that psychic level.

Even when you have psychic abilities going into that level is dangerous because it is tricky and we can never understand all the aspects of it. All of us, abilities or not, need to stay where we are meant to be, and do what we know we should be doing if we are intent on being mentally and emotionally stable and safe.

At the end of the seventh month fat begins to be deposited on your body. You are about fourteen inches long and you weigh from two to four pounds. Your hearing is fully developed and you change your position frequently. You are also responding to many kinds of stimuli, including sound, light, and pain.

"The mother is in much illusion about how she is being with her baby. She considers herself to be a loving mother because she takes time from her busy schedule with her other children to meditate and to focus on her baby. She is doing bonding exercises. This does give the fetus some relief because the mother calms herself and leaves her body slightly."

The most important activity pregnant parents can do is to begin eliminating all conscious (and then subconscious) negative intentions, thoughts, feelings, actions, and interactions from their daily lives together.

"The fetus is intrigued by the energies she sees in people. She is projecting yellow energy outward expressing interest in the energies of people around her. She is also carefully watching her mother's intentions. Her mother is doing the right things, but with possessive intentions. This mother is intent on making her baby more intelligent and versatile than a normal baby. The baby is responding by agreeing to be this way."

"I'm seeing light green energy along with the red. This is also an expression related to physical health and a resulting sense of well-being. This sense of well-being helps the mother emotionally and is beneficial for her baby."

It cannot be stressed enough that the mother's

physical, mental, and emotional conditions are vitally important to the health and well-being of her unborn baby. If a mother is willing to ground herself in the truth that, how she takes care of her body affects her unborn baby, she may be more willing and inclined to make the push to act against selfish drives to indulge in poor eating, overeating, lack of proper exercise, or various seemingly okay desires that she knows are not right.

As I keep saying, understanding is like a great big door to willingness to do what is right. It is much easier to stop negative intentions, thoughts, feelings, and behaviors in general when we realize why we are behaving a certain way, and what our actions mean to those around us. It is also so very important to keep in mind how our negativity impacts on our unborn babies, our newborns, our infants, and our young children.

Although adults don't usually feel the psychic brunt and power of negative energy the way children do, our lives would be so much easier without it. When we look at the following scenarios some may seem understandable. But, they are only understandable when we view our hurtful actions as being "only human." That means that we view our actions as not being seriously wrong so they are basically okay. This gives us lots of room to repeat hurtful behaviors again and again.

We are much more than our definition of only human. We can choose to be any way we want to be, and do. I am convinced that the more we understand our hurtful actions, related to being only human, we will be more willing to recognize our subconscious levels and change our negativity at its source. Here are some examples of only human viewed from the conscious top side as well as the underneath subconscious reality.

"Normally, the mother is 'crazy' and running from one chore to another. The feeling is that she is never going to catch up. She gets frustrated and angry at interruptions from her children and then feels out of control. This kind of stress is difficult for her fetus. The baby feels all of the feelings of her mother."

The mother is going through high and low points and telling herself it is perfectly normal. Her attention is now very much on herself. She is trying to deal with her emotions and stay, what she calls, balanced.

"The father has given up. He feels this is something his wife needs to go through alone. Nonetheless, he does not believe it because she was not this bad when she was pregnant with the boys. He hopes the way she is being will end after the baby is born. He is excited about having a daughter. He thinks that seeing a girl growing up will be fascinating. His wife is acting crazy because she subconsciously knows that her fetus daughter has gone into negative agreement with her husband and she is jealous."

"The baby is (emotionally) crying out. He is in pain. His mother is having cramps and the baby is feeling the stress of her pain. She is having an emotional crisis and is trying to suppress it, so her negative emotional energy is turning into physical pain for her baby."

She is in reaction to her husband feeling a passionate kind of love for his son. She has not experienced this kind of emotional love from him that she is presently witnessing. She is jealous and angry and is trying to hide her feelings by suppressing them. She does not want to show her insanely jealous feelings. This is a big problem for her fetus because when her feelings are suppressed he feels them more intensely.

"The father has been consistently projecting controlling energy (with his thoughts and desires of possession) onto his wife and the baby in her womb. At seven months, I'm seeing that the gold controlling energy is not there in the baby or in the mother at this time. It seems to come and go according to the father's will and mental attitude. The fetus experiences a sense of freedom without his father's controlling energy."

I'm seeing a pale red energy in the womb right now. This indicates a certain kind of vitality that is present when his father has pulled away his psychic control. When the husband pulls back his controlling energy, his wife also feels a freedom and vitality.

The energy restrictions of her husband bring down everyone in the family.

In reading over these excerpts, I started thinking that they are boring, that maybe I should look through my readings and find more interesting examples. As I was doing that I realized that all the readings are mundane and boring! Selfishness is mundane and boring! When we are being selfish our everyday lives become uninteresting and routine, even though most often they are also complicated.

To get relief from ourselves we often build more acceptable lives within our minds and ignore our true realities (as I have been saying). Nonetheless, that unreality, as we already know, only brings a sense of inner insecurity and a searching for happiness and answers. Right choices are the ways to happiness and the answers to all of our insecurities and bad feelings.

At eight months in the womb, you are now in the homestretch! You measure almost 19 inches long from your head to your toes and you weigh as much as five pounds. You are filling the space in your mother's uterus but you may still have enough room to do somersaults. You are probably settling into your head down position, but at this time it may not be your final position.

"I am seeing this fetus experiencing pleasurable physical feelings from the growth process. The growth process produces a strong physical positive energy

and, at times, the baby is enjoying this feeling of health and growth."

"A fetus baby over a three-week period: The fetus is anxious to get out of his environment. His womb space has become cramped, and he cannot move around as much as before. He's blaming his mother for this restriction. His mother seems to be increasingly more agitated, and her baby is feeling that and applying it to his restricted situation.

Two weeks later the baby is still agitated. His body is sore from his mother's abrasive negative energy and he is emotionally and physically worn out. She is also emotionally and physically worn out. All her hostility, suppression, and resistance about this baby as well as her husband are taking a toll.

Three weeks later the mother is anxious to get this over with. Her fetus is sleeping most of the time. He does seem to be inwardly or intuitively preparing for his birth. His inability to move freely about is also sending him inward."

Here is an example of a woman reasoning that her negative feelings are to be expected so late in the pregnancy. With understanding, this kind of a situation can be somewhat relieved. By the time women reach their ninth month, most have had enough and are just waiting for the big day. This is a good time to practice being in present time, not in the future. A woman should do whatever she can for the sake of her baby. The baby comes first. Hire a babysitter for other children or someone to clean the house. Rest, but do whatever you can for your baby, not yourself. This focus will help you be more loving and caring. Even if you feel you can't get over some of your negative feelings, whatever you can do with the purpose of caring for your baby will help everyone involved.

"The baby is picking up on all of her feelings and applying them directly to himself and his situation. He is anxious, not because his womb space has become cramped; he can deal with that just fine. It is his mother's emotional negativity that is difficult.

He has no right answers for his feelings because they are not his own. They belong to his mother. If he were more willing to keep his attention out he would discover that the feelings he is having are coming 'at him' and that would tell him that they are not his own."

Your skin is pink now instead of red and it is less wrinkled. A layer of fat is continuing to form under your skin. This means you will have the body fat reserves you will need to regulate your body temperature once you reach your destination into the world. Your fingernails are extending beyond your fingertips and you are practicing opening your eyes and breathing.

"The baby seems stuck, cramped, and uncomfortable. He is rocking himself to soothe his feelings. He is sleeping more now; in fact, most of the

time. He is drained of energy and feels he does not want to live. He wants to be free of the stress and irritation wearing on him. This is the baby's experience in present time, as he goes into his eighth month in the womb. He does not understand these feelings because they are not his own."

"The mother is being insincere. She is pretending to be happy that the birth is approaching. There is a tremendous amount of suppressed anger and a feeling of depression. She is viewing her negative feelings as a normal part of the pregnancy. She also relates them to her physical condition and her children."

But, the truth is, the baby's mother is angry because she believes her husband is pretending to care about her but has been more distant. She thinks she is doing this pregnancy alone, but from the start she has wanted to do it alone—or, wanted her husband's attention without having to give to him.

"I'm looking at this mother in her eighth month and she is anxious and fidgety. At this moment, she feels as if she has had enough of this pregnancy—she wants it to be over. This entire experience is weighing heavily on her."

Why is she feeling this way right now? It seems to be in relation to her husband. She feels he can do whatever he wants, but he takes pleasure in restricting her actions and interactions. She has been staying home when she would ordinarily be going out with him. For one reason or another, he doesn't want her to go places with him. She feels disheartened. This is a drag. She wants to get it over with so she can get back to normal.

Do you see what I mean about selfishness? These seem to be good, well-meaning people. Aren't they trying to do the best they can with what they've got? No. They are not. How can I say this? Why am I judging people so harshly? Seriously, I am attempting to describe a true reality, although it is a harsh one. You may argue that these occurrences are not nearly as harsh as millions of other acts that are severely harmful.

I would say that they are all on the same plane of our selfish existence. They are all on the *"street of selfishness."* They are all the same in that they are all acts with varying degrees of selfishness. Granted, we never want to go anywhere near the horrific side of the street. The consequences of that would be pure hell; to say nothing of the suffering of those we would be hurting.

Most of us, thankfully, stay on the minimal to medium side of selfishness. But, this does not get us even close to where we could be by making truly right choices every (or almost every) step of the way. This is our tremendous loss in every respect.

If we would allow ourselves to recognize and be wrong about our behavior and correct it every time we made a wrong choice, we would get the knack of it; we would get to see what is truly possible within ourselves and in our immediate life circumstances. Nonetheless, it is a "catch 22." You can't know unless you consistently do it. But if you do it, you are sure you will lose!

What I am attempting to do is to show a way to get off the street of selfishness, not to go from one side of the street to the other. That would be like just staying in the box. We take it for granted that we can't be as we know we should be; we do this knowing full well that we can. I think the problem is that we, early on, start believing the lie that says that we are not able to behave as we know we should. We have many reasons to back up our belief. By enacting this lie <u>we</u> set our own bar; instead of letting what we know is right be the bar.

The crazy thing is no matter what we tell ourselves the bar for Human Beings is always true rightness. We know this; if we didn't we wouldn't need to give ourselves excuses for our actions when we go against what we know is the right thing to do. Right choices are intended to guide us to fulfill our true potential. We will never get there without them.

We are so ingrained in our selfish way of choosing, thinking, and acting that we defend it constantly. If you doubt this observe your thoughts when you make a selfish choice. You can't make a selfish choice, or even think a selfish thought without making an excuse for doing so. Nonetheless, if you can you are probably very far from your core self and would likely not be reading a book like this one.

It is so difficult for us to believe that <u>all</u> choices to intend, think, feel, and act selfishly keep us in mental, emotional, and physical pain of some kind or another. However, we can trace most of our day-to-day psychological and physical aches and pains directly to our selfish or wrong choices. Honest observation is the only way to counter our wrong belief.

Dismantling this belief and coming to the truth that <u>all</u> selfish intentions and acts cause pain is complicated.

We usually blame our mental, emotional, and physical pain on everything but our own selfish choices. It takes much honest introspection to achieve this goal of dismantling. It has to be done in the moment, not being off somewhere meditating. It must be an active ongoing exercise if you want to be truly successful.

It's like going from a C to an A in class. Most of us can't get there without putting in a lot of time and effort. It is the same with right choices. It takes time, effort, and consistency. You will find that there are rewards every step along the way. Once you turn away from a wrong choice, the right choice, and the benefits of it, will become obvious. It is not like a miracle; the right answer and choice were there all along; but in a selfish mode you were not able to see them.

I guess I am talking about when you are willing but you are kind of on the fence, which makes you not totally sure. When we are working to sincerely do the right thing, for most of us in the beginning the "fence" seems to be a daily part-time experience. The more we work consistently the faster we will get off the fence (each time) and the reward of that will push us along. With practice, the process becomes clearer and easier.

When you have taken this path for a while, and you are not doing wrong with blatant knowledge, and really working to do what is right in the moment, the right choices that are less obvious will come up constantly.

It is only when you give up your ideas and what you want in the situation that the right choice will become clear. When this happens, it is a truly heartfelt experience. You will feel grateful. Nonetheless, you cannot have that experience unless you are seriously working to dismantle your selfish intentions as well as your beliefs.

Your brain is working effectively and continuing to develop rapidly. Your memory is active so you will remember your parents' voices as well as events in your immediate surroundings. You can see and hear; and most of your internal systems are well developed. Most of your body's organs are developed except for your lungs. But, by the end of this month, they will be fully matured.

"Grace, the basically fearful fetus, is putting an energy cord out to her sister. The energy cord is in the first and second energy centers. She is saying, 'Stay with me. Help me.' It is as if she's pleading with her sister to take care of her. They are sensing that something is going to change and they're not going to be like this forever. The basically fearful fetus, Grace, is afraid of being totally alone. At least in the womb she has her sister in this energetic connection where they play, do things together, and follow each other. Grace is clinging to that experience and doesn't want to lose it. She is sensing that she is going to lose the physical closeness to her sister. Gwen is saying, 'I will take care of you. You can stay with me.' They understand each other's position."

Gwen understands that her sister is often alone and cut off from her mother and also that her father is not relating to her. Their father is not relating to either one of them so they share this, and they understand how the other feels. They have a bond in this understanding.

"I see the mother is in a much better mental and emotional place than she was before. She may have stopped smoking and does not seem to have the issues that she had earlier. Her anger is much less. Her baby's circulation is better; so is his immune system. Generally, he is in much better health than he was

during the last couple of months. She is feeling that she will be happy when this baby is born. She will be happy to have a family with her husband, and hopefully, their life together will quiet down. The two of them can share a family together with this new baby."

In the next seven weeks, you will be growing faster than you have so far. You will gain more than half your birthweight. By the end of this month you will not be able to move as freely as you have been, so you will curl up with your knees bent. Your head will remain downward. This position allows more blood supply to your brain for development.

"Two siblings are jealous of the fetus baby, and one is happy to have her. The happy child is also in agreement with his mother. He feels the baby will be a relief from his mother's pressure and attention on him. He also feels a connection with the baby and reaches out to her with thought and picture energies. This feels good to the fetus and she responds to the boy."

"I'm seeing the baby becoming increasingly aware of the outside world and especially the mental and emotional reality of his sisters. He is reaching out to the members of his family; reaching out energetically looking for common feelings and common ground. I'm seeing three little energy rays. They're not energy cords. They are energy rays going out to the three

children in his family. This is a form of natural communication. Good feelings are being exchanged between the womb baby and his sisters."

The clarity of these mental and emotional exchanges seemed unbelievable to me at first. However, the more I read pregnant women, when eight and nine months came around, I saw the same interactions again and again. This kind of communication is a very natural occurrence. If an unborn baby is not communicating this way by late in the pregnancy, there is a problem.

"One of his siblings appears a bit hostile and threatened about this communication, but the other two seem happy about it. One sister is really enjoying it. The sister who is nine years old is resistant because having a new baby means that she will have to help her mother more. Because she is the oldest child, this baby will mean added responsibilities and work.

The four-year-old and the younger sister are open to the exchanges going on between them and their baby brother. They are welcoming him. This type of activity seems to be the next stage of womb development. It involves reaching out and communicating with other members of the family besides the mother and father."

For a baby inside the womb, the physical wall of flesh does not separate him from his family. At eight months, a fetus is already mentally and emotionally active in his family. He is experiencing and responding to the family's various energetic realities. He is participating energetically, either by responding to the thoughts and feelings, or avoiding them. He is reading the minds of the family and understanding the relationships and situations in which he is involved. He responds differently to each.

Your body's skeleton is continuing to harden. However, your skull bones will not fuse together because they will overlap during your delivery into the world.

"The mother feels worn out and has arranged for someone to do chores. She is reading books and magazines in bed and taking baths to relax. This is a great help to her fetus."

"I am getting a dull sense. She seems to be sleeping much more now, somehow preparing for birth. She is processing the stress she has been experiencing. She goes almost unconscious for long periods. She seems to be resting and storing up energy for the birth process. This looks like it may be a natural thing."

Now, all the physical activities in and around you are preparing you for your birth. Your mother's antibodies are travelling to your immune system to help in fighting germs after birth. She is also consuming more calcium in her diet to help your skeleton to harden.

"Her husband says she has regressed to being like a teenager. She feels she can get away with it

because she is pregnant. However, for her baby, this is better than suppressing her feelings. Her tantrums are relieving pressure from her baby because she is releasing pent-up energy in her body.

Underneath she is afraid that she has done something terribly wrong and that her baby is going to be deformed or die or might already be dead. She has no assurance from her doctor because she was not honest with him about her eating problem and the fact that she has not been gaining enough weight on purpose. No matter what, she does not want to look fat.

Her guilt is making her feel crazy. She wants to tell the doctor but is terrified and does not want any possible outcome to be her fault."

This is a good example of how we have so many hidden motives, drives, and actions that cause us much fear and sometimes torment. Having the courage to be honest with the people we have meaningful relationships with, will take place one difficult truthful choice at a time; and, it must be done for the sake of all involved.

Our wrong choices are always reactions. They may seem like reactions to our immediate circumstances, which they are, but when analyzed you will find that they will always go back to, and relate to, your reactions to significant events and situations in your home life starting in the womb. Again, this kind of introspection and information will greatly help in minimizing the number of times you react, and the amount of charge in your reactions.

Six
Coming Down the Home Stretch

"If you have been strong in relying on your awareness and innate sense of right, they will continue to guide you through your natural progression to birth."

The big day is fast approaching as you begin your ninth month in your mother's womb. You are intuitively sensing that some big changes are about to occur. If you have been intent upon reading your mother's thoughts you have an idea of what is about to happen. Unfortunately, this can be misleading because of your mother's ideas and feelings about the big event.

Nonetheless, if you are strong in relying on your innate sense of what is happening you will be better able to go through this process step by step as the sensing-knowledge presents itself to you. Your innate sense and awareness of rightness will guide you through the process of your birth.

"Even at nine months into the pregnancy when I met this woman, she was looking and feeling good

physically. This is important. There is good energy here because of this mother's choices and the way she feels about herself."

I have found that many pregnant women often feel unattractive and heavy. How they feel about themselves causes a problem for their unborn babies. A woman will sometimes dress and look bad when she feels down on herself. This makes her feel worse. She has to remember that her baby is at the effect of her feelings. Her baby lives in her emotional atmosphere. When you are pregnant at times you are bound to feel fat, disheveled, or just plain unattractive. That is when you need to pull yourself up by your boot straps, and do what you can to look good, feel good, and get on with your life.

In general, we (men and women) are so easy on ourselves when it comes to allowing ourselves to think and feel in negative ways. We cave in to ourselves with our endless excuses for feeling and acting badly. Believe me, it is so much easier to just do the "bootstrap" thing. Get over yourself as they say these days, and don't allow yourself to go into those places.

Another point is that, alas, we all tend to mentally judge each other by how we look. We pick up on the way people think about us and usually react to their judgments one way or the other. Generally, when you look good, you will feel good, and your baby will benefit from your good feelings.

At nine months, you are continuing to grow and mature. Your lungs are almost fully developed. Your reflexes are now coordinated so you can blink, turn your head, grasp firmly, and respond to outside stimuli.

"This baby is very ready to be a part of his new world. He knows how his mother feels about him. As the time gets closer she is excited. She's feeling love. However, she goes in and out of wanting this baby. Knowingly, the baby responds to her different moods. He is emotionally integrating himself with the family as his birth gets near."

"He is extremely aware of his outer environment and is reaching out energetically as he should be at this time."

Being born seems to be simply a natural progression of the energetic interactions that have been happening in the womb. Birth will mean being with the family outside of the womb.

We don't really get to know what a nine-month-old baby in the womb is thinking and feeling. Our focus is on the pregnant mother: her concerns, her thoughts, fears, and experiences. We tend to forget that this little one is a person with thought processes, feelings, and a wealth of experiences so far.

I've seen so many pictures of a baby right after birth screaming in fear or anger, feeling totally alone and distressed. Somewhere, we don't know what to do, so we ignore the baby's true experience and pretend it is otherwise. Most often we don't know what to do in such a "special" situation so we don't see it clearly. We don't realize the extent of the newborn's distress or pain; we have not realized it for the past months.

We don't think of fetuses in the womb as having human mental and emotional lives. We mostly view their births as the first day of their lives when, in fact, they have been alive for nine months and have had a wealth of positive and negative interactions, events, and experiences.

If we changed our perspective to view an unborn baby as beginning his or her life at conception, that would be a starting point. This would give us the potential ability to see a baby in truth. But, to do that, we would have to change our lives big time.

I say this, not only because of the abortion issue, but we would have to change our perspective across the board. We would have to acknowledge our own subconscious, psychic lives, and know and do all the things I've been talking about so far. We would have to become sensitive to another level of our existence that for most of us seems inaccessible or even nonexistent. But I assure you, it is more accessible than anyone might imagine. All it takes is willingness. As I keep noting, the catch is we have to reverse our selfish choices to get there.

"The mother is angry with her husband. His ownership of the children is really bothering her. Her fetus is now strongly connecting with two of his siblings. He feels that connection as a loving kind of security. The baby is emotionally reaching out, preparing himself to come out into their physical world. He's seeing much more about his family situation in this ninth month. It is almost as if the wall of skin between the baby and the outside world is not even there."

Here are some interesting facts about sibling rivalry. It involves child to parent negative agreements. Typically, you have one basically angry parent and one basically fearful parent as mentioned earlier. In a family with several children, some children will be basically angry and some basically fearful. They will each gravitate toward the parent of similar disposition as their own. Then, guess what? You have sibling rivalry. Some of the children will invariably be in agreement with one parent and some with the other parent. The children in agreement with the same parent will typically be closer, but at odds with the siblings in agreement with the other parent. Another factor is the basically angry, basically fearful dynamic. Siblings with the same basic disposition are usually closer. This is complicated because there are many elements involved.

The facts of the actual agreements and the strength of the agreements contribute to the complexity. A child's actual day-to-day involvement with each parent is also a factor. This can be confusing but, once you know the core reality about basic dispositions and agreements with parents, you can figure out the rest about your own family situation.

By the end of this month, you will measure from 18 to 20 inches long and you will weigh about seven to seven-and-a-half pounds. You are fully developed so you can survive outside of your mother's body.

"This baby is sleeping much more than most of the babies I have clairvoyantly read. It seems natural that a late-term fetus would be looking outward and be energetically communicating and ascertaining information about the family situation of which he will soon be a part. This amount of avoidance and sleeping is not good."

We have much more influence in (and responsibility for) our children's development of learning and behavior than we can imagine or would like to admit. Just because a child is born a certain way does not relieve us of possible fault and responsibility. There are always exceptions, but it would be wise to consider ourselves as the rule and work from there. This is another example of a willingness to be wrong in order to see the actual truth about yourself, or of a person or a situation.

"I'm seeing these babies kicking each other, feeling the space restrictions, irritated, and fighting with one another."

This is a good example of how "human" and complex unborn babies can be when things are not to their liking. They are blaming each other for their space restrictions and reacting. Nonetheless, for several months they have been playing with each other and feeling a close bond, which will return when they stop reacting!

"This fetus does seem lifeless. As I am looking at the baby she seems to be floating, but there is nothing physically wrong. She is emotionally dull and is not looking out or reaching out. She seems to be in a sleep state right now, but even when babies in the womb sleep, they energetically reach out and are responding and interacting in different ways. It is almost as if this baby is in a state of shock."

Again, it seems that we do not take responsibility for the mental and emotional conditions of our babies before or after they are born. If we ever get to incorporate the subconscious psychic level of our existence into our conscious awareness, we will have to make a baby's mental, emotional, and physical condition a part of our concerns and responsibilities. Nonetheless, if we are not willing to take responsibility for our children's mental, emotional, and physical conditions we will never get to know our own subconscious self or that of our children's. It is that "catch 22" again.

Your skin is pink and smooth. You have permanently settled lower in your mother's abdomen to prepare for birth. The placental blood flow is increasing dramatically to support your rapid growth. The placenta itself is growing as well.

"When the baby goes outward and tunes in to her mother she feels her mother's instability and craziness, then, she retreats inward. When she goes out to the father, the father is, I'm getting the words, 'fed-up' and he has had enough of this woman. He has had enough of this marriage. He has had enough of this pregnancy and now he is ignoring the baby. That is also why the baby is inward.

This seems to be temporary with the father, but it has been ongoing since his wife has been acting out so dramatically. This father is feeling more and more at his wits' end as to what to do with his wife. He believes the only things he can do is wait until she has the baby and then see what happens."

It seems that this father is sincerely trying to make this situation better. He has been doing everything he can think of to make his wife feel better, but without success. He loves her but is strongly attached. Because he is not willing to put anything on the line, he has no leverage. It is not that he should be threatening her, but he is afraid of losing her so he won't challenge her "*craziness*" and her wrong choices. He complains but will not deal with the situation rightly because of his fear of losing her. She seems to be in full control of the marriage because she knows he will do almost anything she wants. She knows she can have it her way, which is usually not the right way.

"The mother has toned down her anger and is insecure. She has made this pregnancy a mostly negative experience. The baby is inward, hiding within herself, and withdrawing from her mother's energy. This fetus has rarely had her attention out during her time in the womb. She will be inward like her father. It is extremely difficult for the baby to look out and put her attention outward. She feels a deep sense of confusion and heaviness.

The father is excited and happy. He wants a baby to take care of, but is worried about his girlfriend's volatility and possessiveness. There is no reason to believe that this baby will have an easier time of it after she is born. She will be quite the same unless her circumstances change, or she changes in relation to them."

They say it takes a village to raise a child. I don't know about that, but I do know it takes a selfless mother and father to properly care for and guide a child, starting when he or she is in the womb. It takes both parents working it out and challenging each other on what they see and sense is wrong in each other and the relationship. They need to do this without blame and with the sincere intent of making life easier and more caring for all involved, especially the baby about to be born.

"She is becoming much like her mother. She is drawing everything to herself. This started when she became able to hear sounds. She would draw the sounds toward her instead of following, going outward, and discovering what the sounds were about like a normal fetus baby. The father is concerned about the baby. The baby is feeling that concern and her father's fear. She is going inward in reaction to her mother's instability."

I think that, if we could get past our disbelief of the truth about the psychological sophistication of babies in the womb and know that they are capable of mental and emotional interaction, reaction, and pain, we would be willing to change our lives, and ourselves for their benefit.

"This fetus seems content. He has been looking out, he seems to know what to expect, and somehow knows that he will be with his brothers. His father wanted a girl but a boy seems okay too. This baby seems to be healthy and developing emotionally without much negative energy impacting on him. This is something I do not often see. The emotionally healthy environment relates to the father and mother wanting a family and wanting this baby. Also, their attentions are usually

where they should be: on the right things to do, not on themselves."

These parents are not extremely selfish like many parents I have read. They are not impacting negatively in extreme ways on their unborn baby. They are not having the subconscious selfish reactions and self-seeking desires that I find to be typical. Both this baby and mother seem ready for the birth, another unusual observation.

"The baby is picking up fear from her mother. The mother is afraid her husband is going to steal the baby's affections. She has no confidence that her baby will love her. The fetus has not been looking out much and because of this is not developing mentally as she should."

"After she is born, she will probably be inward and slow to learn. She has been this way for the past five months in the womb. This is mainly in reaction to her mother restricting her with energy when she attempts to look out or reach out to her father."

Sometimes a child's inability to learn, speak, interact, or any number of other mental, emotional, and physical problems is like "the elephant in the living room." We just refuse to see what is really going on because, for some reason, we are just terrified of having to take responsibility for any wrongdoing. I know that I do keep repeating myself, but so do the selfish events that I'm addressing.

"As the birth date is approaching this mother is getting really 'crazy.' She is acting in juvenile ways and her husband does not know what to do with her. He never dreamed she would be going over the edge and getting out of touch with reality. He was not prepared for this, and it is scaring him. He cannot wait for the pregnancy to be over so he can see if she is going to get back to normal."

"As the birth approaches, the father is getting visibly excited. His excitement is threatening his wife and she is suppressing her fear. The mother is also suppressing anger about her husband's happiness. The baby is greatly at the effect of her mother's fear and inner volatility."

Jealousy and possession are a huge part of selfish behavior. Jealousy and possession are two selfish reactions that are usually deep, and when strong, relate back to sexual abuse by one or both parents. However, reactions to all abusive actions create patterns that are deep-seeded and lasting. They seem impossible to get rid of, even when we desperately want to have them gone forever.

I would like to end this chapter with a perspective that may be helpful in our attempts to change subconscious and hidden intentions, ideas, desires, and actions that we may not yet have the courage or the willingness to change.

The following analogy and comparison may give additional light to the truth about the design and magnificence of our humanness.

A while ago I came across a physical exercise theory and technique that parallels what I have found to be true on the spiritual/subconscious/psychic/psychological level of our humanness. It is called "*Pilates*," discovered by Joseph Pilates, who wrote a book about it in 1945.

It has only been in the last couple of decades that many physical trainers have come to discover and understand the Pilates theory and method of exercise. The theory is that our physical core muscles determine how our exterior muscles will respond. When a person exercises his or her core muscles properly, physical problems can be cured or lessened and a greater level of strength, flexibility, and balance can be achieved. Your core muscles are your abdominal muscles, the essential spinal and back muscles, the muscles in your pelvic floor and the diaphragm.

To the extent that your core physical muscles are healthy your exterior muscles work properly. When they are weak or not functioning properly the rest of your body is weak and you typically have a variety of physical problems. All these muscles are your foundation for movement and balance. Many cannot be seen because they are buried underneath other muscles. However, they all work together to keep your trunk stable. For instance, if your core spinal muscles were severely damaged, you would not be able to sit up without holding on to something. You would just topple over.

I would say that our spiritual core muscles are the spiritual equivalent of our physical core muscles. Your spiritual core muscles are your subconscious intentions and choices.

Our subconscious intentions and choices are not as hidden as our physical core muscles are, because we can choose to see and know them any time we are willing. How we choose to exercise our spiritual (subconscious) core muscles determines our every positive and negative conscious intention, thought, feeling, action, and reaction.

To the extent that your spiritual core muscles are healthy, your behavior and your psychological experience and outlook will be stable and truly positive.

However, when your subconscious and hidden intentions and choices are negative, wrong, and selfish, your character and personality will reflect those choices. Invariably you will experience and display a variety of psychological problems.

As properly exercising our physical core muscles determines our physical health, balance, and movement by rightly exercising our spiritual core muscles we determine the health of our psychological condition and the amount of well-being we will possess.

Making right choices with your physical core muscles can reverse and cure physical conditions, even serious ones. I believe that the same is true of your spiritual core muscles. It is possible to lessen and even reverse psychological dysfunctions by rightly exercising our spiritual core muscles.

Just as your physical core muscles are the foundation for your physical stability, your spiritual core muscles are the foundation for your psychological stability.

We could be so much more than we are if we would only choose for it! As you can see in most of the excerpts, selfish choices deprived so many normal, everyday people of intimacy and the happiness that comes with true love and caring.

Seven
Changing Gears for a Moment

"An unborn baby's awareness and ability to choose have been documented repeatedly by medical scientific research and published reports."

At this juncture, I would like to change gears somewhat and talk about doubt, scientific facts, and simple human reasoning. For anyone still not convinced of the psychological sophistication of unborn babies and the typically difficult mental, emotional, and physical time they have in the womb, I would like to reiterate some scientific facts that I consider to be empirical evidence. I would also like to comment on those facts and give some reminders and new perspectives.

Most of us don't think about what a baby might be thinking and feeling at birth or before. Some think that babies are blank slates and at birth they begin to develop psychologically. Yet, scientific research states that at five months in the womb a fetus has mental activity and does dream. By the time of birth he or she has developed an individual personality.

Brainwave tests can pick up periods of REM sleep. This indicates a dream state, and dreaming signifies thinking and the processing of images that have meaning to the fetus. While sleeping, facial expressions and body movements show whether the unborn baby is having a pleasant or an unpleasant sleep experience.

What is dreaming? Don't we process thoughts and feelings when we dream? What are the fetuses processing? What are they dreaming about? They are dreaming about and processing their thoughts, feelings, and experiences of the day, just as we do. They are reliving and processing their memories of images and feelings.

Unborn babies make choices, think, feel, remember, hear, learn, and react in positive or negative ways.

Studies show that babies in the womb have a lot to learn and a lot to deal with; they think, feel, and react or respond in positive and negative ways. It is difficult for us even to imagine that babies being born would even be able to think, much less have the mental and emotional complexity they do have. But, what are the other possibilities? Are they blank slates? Do they not think at all? Do they just not know things? Most of us don't think about it, don't really wonder what, if anything, is going on in their heads. Some think that the older they get the smarter they get, or the more aware they become. Some believe that they start at nothing and then start developing.

What we previously believed has been proven false by medical scientific research. In addition, I have clairvoyantly sensed and believe that even in the earliest stage of an embryo, intelligence is present. As the embryo grows and develops, the Human Being is better able to manifest through that human body.

What is mental activity? Isn't it thinking? If you are thinking you must be thinking something specific. That is the way thinking works. You can't be thinking abstractly or about nothing. Any thought that we might consider being abstract is a thought that we are not fully focused on. That involves our attention, not the thought itself.

Some people claim that in meditation they can quiet their minds and not be thinking. That is impossible. No matter how calm we can get, there is always thought, conscious as well as subconscious. So, babies *do* think about *something*. Wouldn't you be curious to know about that certain momentary something?

If you are thinking, aren't you feeling? Doesn't thought create emotional feeling? Fetuses and babies emotionally feel concerning whatever it is they are thinking and experiencing. They are thinking about what they are discovering in the womb and about themselves in relation to that; they are thinking and evaluating what they feel from their mothers and fathers.

Because initially unborn babies only perceive what is true and respond to it, I believe that their thinking is simple. It becomes more complicated as they react and respond and invariably cloud some of their ability (willingness) to intuit, see, and respond. This ability is rooted in a baby's innate ability to be aware and to freely choose for or against what is right, true, loving and lovingly responsible. As you know, I believe this ability was up and running at conception.

An unborn baby's awareness and ability to choose have been repeatedly documented by medical scientific research and published reports.

A fetus will visibly respond when a bright light is shone on the outside of his or her mother's stomach. Some babies move toward the light and fixate on it, others move away from the light seemingly disturbed by it. In reacting to the light, the fetus is demonstrating his or her ability to see objects in space and respond to them in a determined and coordinated way.

Nonetheless, you don't have to be a doctor or go to school to know the truth about babies. This is who we are; this is what we presently experience. They are like us, only little and a lot less complicated. Typically, we can't really imagine what a five-month-old fetus is thinking or feeling. So, in the back of our minds, we conclude that they are not thinking anything.

Ignoring the truth does not make it go away. It may feel like a safer way to go, but we always know subconsciously what we are doing and what is going on within ourselves and with those we love. When a baby is born and we see him or her as a beautiful little "bundle of joy" we are, for the most part, in great illusion. We have the beautiful part right, but there is so much more going on that we don't want to see. The newness of life is a joy. To hold a newborn or an infant gives you a sense of wonder and makes you feel alive, but that is what *you* are feeling. All too often it is not what the baby is thinking, feeling, and experiencing.

To know a baby's experience from moment to moment our full attention must be on the baby, not on our ideas about the baby, and not on how the baby makes us feel. That goes for positive as well as negative thoughts and feelings. It is easy to feel good and be in illusion when the baby seems content; and it is easy to get frustrated or upset when the baby is having a problem. Either way, we are in our ideas about our baby and that is in no way helpful. Without this baggage, you could be able to see the baby's mental and emotional state in that moment.

This seems to be a very "inconvenient truth". In order to see your baby in truth, as he or she is in the moment, you have to be willing to see, not only the truth in that moment, but, the truth in general. This takes work, as I keep saying. Nonetheless, this is another big incentive for us to work on giving up ideas to see the reality of the present moment.

However, knowing your baby in the moment does not have to be a down-the-road thing; your practice should be with the object involved. In this case it is your baby. In the moment, you can sincerely ask to see what is really going on, and you may be very surprised by the answer and what might happen next. I'm not thinking of anything specific. It is just that when we sincerely look for the truth, and we want to do the right thing, it seems that we are always surprised because something comes up that we have not considered, never expected, and sometimes could not have even imagined.

If you can get yourself into a place of contentment your baby will miraculously calm down and feel peaceful, no matter what his or her condition. Our biggest problem is that our peaceful loving state must be real, and that takes consistent right choices. That does not happen overnight.

There is one very hard fact. That is, you are who you have made yourself to be. If you are not a genuinely loving and caring person, in most cases, your baby will have a problem with the feel of you. You can't fool your baby. You can't turn true love on and off. You can't be truly loving and frustrated, anxious or upset at the same time. We all need to work on this consistently and, as I said, it does not happen overnight.

Having said that, as far as our babies are concerned we have to genuinely do the best we can. I say genuinely because *"I did the best I could"* is something we usually say when we feel deeply guilty because we know we were wrong. We say this when we see a problem, or problem child, that is our responsibility and we know we could have and should have done differently.

Living is not easy, and on top of that we don't take our lives and choices seriously. Most of us have absolutely no idea of the amount and nature of pain and confusion we have created for ourselves and those in our charge. I don't really believe the typical version of heaven and hell, but there is one thing I feel certain about. Living or dead, you live the mental and emotional life you have chosen and continue to choose in this life and the next.

Some have said, *"You die the way you have lived."* I think this is true, not only at death but thereafter. I don't think we automatically lose all the mental and emotional consequences of our choices, good or bad, when we die. I think we carry whatever we have created within ourselves, our character, if you will, with us to another realm. Also, we are drawn to and live with like energies, the same as we do in this human realm. I don't really know what the afterlife is all about, but I do know that we have no conscious idea of the importance of our choices. No idea of what we are creating for ourselves when we make wrong choices, especially serious ones. I did not plan this little excursion, but it does seem to be an appropriate addition.

Obviously, medical researchers are not clairvoyant so they could not have the ability to know the substance of a baby's thoughts and feelings. Nonetheless, they, with undeniable evidence, have discovered that an unborn baby thinks, remembers, learns, etc. They have amassed much evidence regarding their research.

An unborn baby will prefer sweet to bitter. Unborn babies listen all the time. Scientists can observe a baby's body dancing to the rhythm of his or her mother's voice, also to music. At first, fetuses are startled by a loud noise, but in time they learn to discriminate and ignore certain routine noises in their surroundings.

Do we need more proof that they really are just like us, with all of our abilities that only need to be further expressed as their physical bodies develop?

The psychological research studies on how an unborn baby turned out give a good indication of what might have been going on with the babies while they were in the womb.

A mother's attitude had the greatest effect on how her baby turned out. Women, who consciously and subconsciously wanted their babies, had the easiest pregnancies and births. They also tended to have the healthiest children, both physically and emotionally.

Subconsciously is a key word here because it is the subconscious that an unborn baby relates to and experiences. Indirectly these scientific medical and psychological experts are, in their way, saying what I have been saying about the subconscious and about babies in the womb. All babies in the womb respond dramatically to positive and negative interactions and circumstances. You can be sure that an unborn baby will never reject true loving intentions and choices.

Many birth dramas are selfishly created during pregnancy and at birth, and they are totally unnecessary. Many of the difficult births and C-sections (that were required because of stress or a long labor) had to do with one simple thing: selfishness. That is, women who were enacting negative patterns and exaggerated self-concern. I don't mean to be picking on women with this comment. Any well-meaning woman, who had been in the situation I just described, would be grateful for the comment. Our biggest mistake is that we keep repeating our mistakes.

Once a baby is born and starts on his or her journey outside of the womb, the drama does not automatically end. If (or it could be when) a baby is not feeling love from a mother or father the days at home may be traumatic. The baby may develop many simple infant psychical problems. At these times, it would be well to consider the psychological side, because typically there is one. I'm not saying don't seek physical solutions and cures, that is totally necessary. But, typically there is an emotional problem underneath a physical problem that is often much more important, and when addressed the physical will most likely resolve itself.

I think all, or the majority of, babies have some problems. Your baby is attempting to adjust to his or her new environment outside of the womb. He or she is learning and dealing with many new circumstances, and old ones as well. I can't stress enough how a parent's behavior (genuine thoughts and feelings) with the baby (and in general) dramatically affect the baby's emotional and physical experience.

It is also important to know that a baby's experience is not really from day to day; it is from moment to moment. The more moments of genuine love (minus negative thoughts, feelings, and stress) the healthier the baby will be both emotionally and physically.

I would like to interject a note here about a misconception that I believe causes much pain for both new mother and baby. That is the concept of postpartum depression or "baby blues." This nickname is a good example of making something very negative and hurtful into something normal and okay. Normal simply means the norm; it does not mean natural. Feeling down and depressed after the baby is born, unfortunately, is probably the norm; but it is very far from being natural. It is self-serving and destructive for both mother and baby. This is a time when it is most important to have your attention off yourself and on your baby. This is not the time to stop being vigilant about making right, loving, truthful, and lovingly responsible choices.

No matter how many people and professionals make this kind of behavior natural and okay, it <u>definitely</u> is not. Just look at it in the light of your baby and you will certainly agree with me. Joy comes in giving. It comes in truly loving without concern for self. Depression is very far in the opposite direction. You may feel worn out, but when you are being truly giving and loving you will find right and loving ways to solve whatever personal problems you may be having.

Statistics say that 70 to 80 percent of women suffer from postpartum depression. The 20 to 30 percent that do not have that problem tell us the truth. Twenty or thirty women out of one hundred women choose to make loving sacrifices for their babies and experience the psychological results of their right choices. That is the way it works in every instance of our lives.

The unexpressed psychological state of a pregnant woman is crucial to the mental, emotional, and physical well-being of her unborn baby.

Here is another bit of scientific evidence relating to what I have been describing in the excerpts from my clairvoyant readings. The unexpressed not only means the subconscious, but literally means what we think and feel consciously and refuse to express about for one reason or another. Our self-interested choices will not help to put us on the road that most of us want to travel. I believe that most of us want to love more, especially our children. But, sadly, with our many complicated patterns and our conscious and subconscious choices of behavior, it seems to be an extremely difficult and complicated road to take—even when we feel that we really want to take it.

The attitudes and choices of fathers are also significant. Fathers who hold negative attitudes and make choices to control, own, or possess their babies consistently emit coercive and hurtful energies that are disturbing and painful to their unborn babies.

Sadly, no one seems to talk about the obvious negatives. This is a significant fact about fathers that is backed by scientific evidence. As far as I can see, for the most part, it has been ignored. Nonetheless we don't need scientific evidence for us to know what we are negatively doing and why, but we could use such information for clarity and as a reminder. Why _not_ talk about it?

To change substantially and truly we need to work on eliminating the negatives. We can't do it the way we often try to do it. We cannot put conscious positive choices and feelings over wrong intentions and choices to enact destructive patterns and expect to be essentially more positive.

Fathers greatly influence their babies in positive and negative ways. It is important for fathers to know that they have a direct relationship with their babies even when their babies are in the womb. However, in order for fathers to truly acknowledge that relationship, they would also have to claim the responsibility they have for the mental and emotional lives of their unborn babies.

Here we have that "catch 22" again. To truly love your child, you need to take full responsibility for all your conscious and subconscious choices. That is not only with your child, it is all across the board. When that becomes a reality, there will not be all the subtle enactments of negative patterns between parents about their babies in the womb. There will not be the hidden jealousy or feeling left out, no subtle possession, or wanting the baby to love you, or love you more. For the men, no thinking that mother and child have a special relationship that you just have to sit back and watch!

This brings up another point, the notion that a woman is miraculously loving when it comes to her baby. That would be a wonderful thing, but sad to say, it is not true. Women don't have an automatic right choice or loving attitude button that makes them essentially or naturally different from men. Straying from this truth can only create illusion, and also stress for women because we know that it is a lie. Sometimes our children can trigger our negative intentions, thoughts, and feelings more than anyone else!

Awareness and choice are great equalizers. Men and women have the same basic abilities to be aware of what is right and to choose for it. Women are not better at this than men, even when it comes to their children. Some women hate and abuse their children just as there are men who hate and abuse their children. Of course, we have the extreme where some men (in relation to the majority) historically kill, rape, and conquer. These atrocities are most often beyond belief. But, I am talking about you and me, us normal folk, who are trying to live in loving and caring ways.

So, women, you don't have to hide your negative intentions and feelings about your unborn babies and other children. Express them and change them. You don't have to pretend or worry about not being a good mother. You *know* when (and if) you are being a good mother and you *know* when (and if) you are not.

Nonetheless, if you want your children's true love and respect you need to earn it by working on lessening and eliminating your negatives.

Studies on schizophrenic and psychotic pregnant women and their babies show the terrible psychological effects that extreme negative mental and emotional energies can have on an unborn baby.

The researchers did not directly mention a baby's choice about their psychological conditions. However, in my view, it seems that it would be tremendously difficult for a baby to make the right choices necessary, to become mentally healthy on his or her own, without the help of at least a normal amount of caring from a mother and father.

Before diving into the birth excerpts, I would like to end this chapter by talking about what the birth might mean for baby and mother and give some insights from my clairvoyant perspective.

The event of birth is a continuation of the natural process of development the fetus has been going through already. The baby carries with him or her (in memory) all the psychic-energetic interactions that have previously occurred. If those exchanges were primarily truly positive, the birth and infancy are likely to be similarly positive; the opposite is also true.

Every baby about to be born has a part to play in his or her birth. Each baby possesses a natural, innate ability to go with the flow of what is happening when the contractions start and the birth process becomes a reality. The baby participates in this process in positive or negative ways.

When babies are being true to their natures, their attentions are out and they are in-tune and know exactly what is happening. It is not that they know what to do ahead of time; rather they have the innate, intuitive awareness of what is occurring in the moment. They can accept that reality or choose to resist it, by becoming fearful or angry in reaction to their new (and old) situation. The baby's choices at this time will most likely reflect the kinds of choices he or she has been making so far.

Also, during the contractions and birth, a pregnant woman, typically, will put little or no attention on the possible physical and emotional state of her baby, and what the baby might be going through. When a mother has total attention on herself, it can leave her baby feeling panicked and alone. Birth can be a relatively pleasant happening when a baby and mother are in a willing and accepting disposition, and not fighting the birth process by being in a reactive state of anger or fear.

Reading about births online, I found that currently the percentages of birth complications of various kinds seem to be high. This would correlate with what I have found to be true in my clairvoyant readings.

I know there are exceptions in physical birth complications but, all too often, birth complications are simply a manifestation of the psychological state of mother and baby.

When a baby is in reaction to prior experiences in the womb he or she is not able (willing) to assess the situation accurately and will often go into panic mode. Also, when a mother is having a difficult time physically and emotionally, the baby will also suffer. These factors contribute to complications and a difficult birth.

It is a tough transition from the womb into the air world. The baby must work to breathe, to eat, and the environment is bright and noisy. There is a hard surface and no fluid to move around in, to say nothing of the emotional trauma often instigated by the baby's parents' subconscious fears and concerns.

From the get-go, we should determine that we will experience our babies as they truly are, not as we imagine them to be.

Essentially, babies act and react as we do; and their essential consciousness is the same. It does not grow and develop as their bodies grow and develop. A baby's choices have much to do with the psychological (mental and emotional) environment in which they find themselves. They respond well to loving attention and react with anger, fear, and confusion when faced with hurtful intentions and choices in relation to them. When a mother has a truly right relationship with her pregnancy, her baby, and the birth, it is probable that both mother and baby will have an easy time during the birth.

Although a baby has free choice (psychologically) from the beginning, the baby's choices most often are in reaction to how he or she is being treated.

This fact gives parents a tremendous responsibility for their child's well-being and life experiences while in the womb, as they grow up, and on into adulthood.

I would like to talk about some of the babies I have clairvoyantly read to give an idea of what many babies may be going through. The excerpts in the next chapter may seem incredible, but I assure you I didn't make them up! (Incidentally, I did the readings on babies in the womb as part of a project in 1992-93. The scientific medical knowledge we now have was not available at that time. I knew what I was seeing was true, but at the time, I was not willing to publish it.)

The psychological sophistication of unborn babies is really something most of us cannot even imagine. But, I think it would behoove us to start. If you can imagine it, you can tune-in to it. If you are open to believing it, your unborn child or infant will benefit. It is when we refuse to know what is going on with them that the situation is at its worst. To know that truth can be a consolation, even when it is bad news. We often refuse to know because it will reflect badly on us, or we will be pained at the knowledge, or we will be confused because we don't know what to think about what they may be going through. If you will note, all these ideas and attitudes are self-serving with no thought of the baby.

Getting to know what your baby may be thinking, feeling, and experiencing in this way is like going into uncharted waters. You can't be certain. You don't really know. Maybe you're wrong. Maybe you know that you will imagine the worst. Or, maybe you tell yourself that you will imagine the best, and then fear being in illusion. When you try to do this, it can be enormously disconcerting. It can be awfully unsettling not knowing if you are, in fact, right or not.

If you are willing to begin this journey with an unborn baby or an infant, your sincere intention to know the truth will move you along. As I said before, you will be surprised and you will get better at it; and, you will find yourself feeling grateful for the information. The truth is always a healer, no matter what that truth may be, even when it is painful. The truth keeps us secure and stable in realness.

You will feel grateful to know how you are hurting your baby with your subconscious choices for self over rightness or your baby. You will feel grateful because you will, simultaneously, have the willingness to change that certain way of being. In a word, you will come to a totally new and unusual way of living and interacting with your baby—and with your life in general.

Moreover, if you don't have a baby, you can still use this process to know more truth about yourself and others, as I have been describing here and earlier in this book. But, a word of caution: Do this only with yourself for a long time before you try to do it with anyone else. I say this because there are many pitfalls along the way. It is much easier to practice on yourself, rather than risk misjudging or hurting others.

Here are points about the circumstances of some babies just before and during birth. If a baby has had a difficult birth, or a birth with complications, in almost every case, he or she will have had one or more of the following experiences.

When unborn babies do not experience genuine love from their mothers or fathers, it can lead to a deep sense of insecurity and a feeling of not being wanted. They fear they will not be properly taken care of and nurtured. These are sense-feelings and images not thinking the way we know it.

Some fetuses close off and withdraw from the angry energies of a mother who is not happy about the pregnancy and birth.

A mother's fearful or angry thoughts and feelings can inhibit a baby from following the intuitive knowledge available to him or her during birth.

Some fetuses lose a sense of self and how to be with their birth processes. The baby will perceive his or her situation as a confused upheaval. This happens because the baby is not willing to trust his or her circumstances.

Such a baby will feel that his or her current situation is not right. However, this is because the baby wants to be in control and cannot control this happening. Many babies, when being fearful or angry, become disoriented and incoherent as soon as the contractions start.

Were a baby to stop trying to control and to resist the physical changes, the baby would go through the birth process in an accepting and easier way. That means he or she would have to stop reacting. The reactions typically include resistance because the baby is not reading the "signals" correctly, and that often results in an angry or a panicked reaction.

Many babies about to be born feel desperate. They are not correctly measuring the truth about their births. Many quickly retreat inwardly and don't ascertain that there is nothing to fear. They become contained within themselves and caught up in their panic and images.

The external disturbances created by the physical changes during birth often trigger inner confusion about the event. This occurs when a baby is panicked about losing control.

Many babies become fearful anticipating what might happen next. These reactions cloud their natural clairvoyant ability to see clearly and respond in the moment. Reaction clouds their awareness of the truth of what is taking place.

Their sense of loss of control and their confusion about their lack of intuitive sensing make these babies feel as if they were dying, rather than being born. They wrongly sense their lives are being taken away or being squeezed out of them.

Babies will most often blame their mothers for their fear, confusion, and pain. When a mother is screaming, crying, or carrying on during the birth it will confirm the baby's beliefs about his or her pain, confusion, and panic.

Many babies are born angry about their new physical circumstances. They react to the negative ideas and feelings of both their parents, especially to the ideas and feelings that relate directly to them.

Resisting their births drives babies to psychologically disconnect from this important next step in their lives: entry into the air world.

When babies rebel against the natural push toward the birth canal, many become physically rigid. Then they mentally and emotionally start fighting. When they fight their exit from the womb they cause confusion and incoherence within themselves.

During the birth process, they may choose to start expressing much of their pent-up angry feelings at the way their mothers or fathers have been treating them.

An unborn baby's panicked and angry reactions disrupt his or her natural clairvoyant ability to see clearly, and this affects the baby's willingness to act rightly.

Many of these choices, experiences, and conditions are not a constant. A baby will most often go in and out of some of these places. Sadly, if a baby is strongly angry or afraid, his or her painful condition will often last for the entire birthing and frequently throughout his or her life. If you look, I think you can see correlations in adult behavior, specifically with the mentally ill. They have many of our unhealthy traits, only more severe and on a sustained basis.

Essentially, we are all equal. But, on a day-to-day basis, our choices for or against rightness make us *unequal.* Just as we have *"basic human rights,"* we have *"basic human psychological abilities and basic human responsibilities."* Our basic human responsibilities come with our innate abilities to see rightness and act on it. That is why, when we deny that responsibility, we inevitably suffer in one way or another.

What makes us different, and sometimes extremely different, and unequal, is how we choose to use our basic human psychological abilities.

In my opinion, the more unequal we feel, or in truth, are, on the downside—the more we want to try to build ourselves up to convince ourselves and others that we are a way that we are not. Also, if we are confident that we are good, it is time to look again. It is important to come from a place of true humility when it comes to measuring ourselves. Look for where you are not doing what is right in all the little things, and change them. Competing with others to show them how good we are is a measure of our dishonesty; this has somehow become an epidemic in these times of the importance of self. As I keep saying we are all the same. We simply differ in what we intend and how we choose. Some of us have chosen very badly, but we still have the moment to moment ability to choose rightly. We are all equal in our innate and essential abilities to know what is right and to choose for it; there are no exceptions! Where we differ is only in how we use those two innate and essential abilities. Unfortunately, that "only" can be, and all too often, <u>is huge.</u>

Eight
The Big Event

"Every baby, about to be born, has a part to play in his or her birth. All babies possess the ability to participate in positive or negative ways."

Let's jump right into the real-life stories of our fetus babies at the time of birth. I'm going to focus on the psychological. At this point, it is all about what the baby is going through mentally and emotionally. In comparison, the physical has a smaller part to play. As I said, when there are complications, it almost always relates to the psychological state of mother and baby.

I'm going to begin with the more positive and less difficult births. According to doctors that would be about twenty to thirty percent! As I went through my readings to choose birth excerpts that I wanted to recount, I realized that this percentage was about right in measuring the total of my fetus clairvoyant readings.

As I said before, the 20 to 30 percent show that these positive accounts are truly possible for all women, when they are willing to put themselves aside and do what is right in the moment. However, there also needs to be previous right and loving choices. Humans could change on a dime, but it would be highly unlikely. Also, without the willingness we will not even see the right thing to do, much less do it.

I'm going to have the accounts run on longer and let them speak for themselves (unless I can't help myself!). If you intently focus on these accounts you may be able to understand what the babies were experiencing. If you tune-in to the babies as you read, you may be able to feel what they were going through. Also, I'm sure most of us can relate to the thoughts, feelings, and behaviors of many of the parents.

Many of these more positive babies have been paying attention to their innate sense of what they should be doing from moment to moment. They obviously have made many right choices with the help of their parents. *"I'm seeing blue energy. It's a certain kind of knowing. He does instinctively know that he is being born and instinctively also knows what to do."*

"The baby seems to be preparing himself for his birth into the physical world, not only physically, but also, psychologically. He is able to see and sense energies, see different colors, and feel and see the thoughts and emotions in these energies."

"This baby is emotionally integrating himself more and more as his birth approaches. He is very

aware of his outer environment and is reaching out energetically as he should."

"Even though there are many underneath dynamics happening, the fetus has a clear womb space in which to mentally, emotionally, and physically prepare for birth. I see the baby responding to the mother who is feeling excited about the birth."

"The baby's father was the first to hold her. His heart went out to her, and he felt a connection. *When he held her, the baby felt a relief and a sense of gratitude. She felt secure and her confusion began to vanish. Being inundated with irritating energy was absent, and this was a great relief. She was relaxing, which was a rare happening. In the womb, she was under her mother's constant pressure and stress, now she felt the absence of that and was feeling her father's caring. When the baby was given to her mother the baby panicked. That old feeling of hostility was back. In fear, she went inside and went to sleep as she would do in the womb."*

"It looks like the baby is having a relatively easy time in the womb. Her parents do not seem to want something for their child strongly. The baby seems content and somehow senses that the birth is about to happen."

"This looks like a light pregnancy and situation, as far as emotions and reactions and the underlying subconscious dimensions are concerned."

"The baby was feeling pressure being pushed out of the womb. His attention stayed outward and he was grounded in his body and the birth process. This outward stance helped him tremendously. He knew the direction he was headed and seemed to know what was going on. He seemed to be aware that he was on his way to being outside of his mother. He did not panic. His presence and awareness made this an easy birth. He slid through the birth canal and out in just moments. The doctor and nurses were excited that it went so fast and easy.

***As I'm looking at this I see that this is the way birth could be all the time**—that is, if a mother isn't resistant and closed, and her baby keeps his or her focus outward, remaining aware and willing to participate. What seemed to be a blessing should be considered as a normal event. But, from what I have seen so far, most births are needlessly difficult. This baby felt a great sense of relief being in the clear air space."*

***"This baby's birth was like an explosion**. He almost shot out. His mother was having contractions and barely made it to the hospital in time. This birth was much easier than her first. I do not think she had medication. The birth was a great relief for both mother and child."*

"The baby came quickly without much trauma. He came so quickly that the mother did not have a

chance to have anesthesia. That was helpful for the baby. Genuine feelings are welcoming this baby. His mother was relieved that the birth happened so fast. She could not believe it was so easy. I'm asking if there was any emotional trauma. I'm getting that there was some trauma. Birth is often traumatic in some way for the baby. I'm going to look at this baby's experience.

I see that this mother was feeling afraid just before the birth, and her baby was picking up on her fears. She was afraid that she might not make it to the hospital in time. She was grateful that the birth was over quickly and her baby was okay. She was worn out, but happy and content to have her baby with her. This mother's feelings are genuine. She is laidback and exhausted. There is not much emotionally going on, which is good. So many times I have read mothers who appeared happy and positive on top, but had much underneath negativity in relation to their babies."

"This birth is fairly easy and short. The baby stayed focused inwardly for most of the birth, as if she was asleep. Yet, she was feeling bombarded by the contractions because she was afraid of what was happening and not sensing it clearly."

Keep in mind, while reading the following more difficult recounts of babies being born, that doctors tell us that there are usually some kinds of complications (from mild to severe) in most births. What I was clairvoyantly seeing and describing in the more difficult births were the psychological underneath parts; sadly, these psychological parts are what have been greatly discounted and ignored.

Here is an example of an unnecessary trauma. *"This pregnancy was nothing like the mother thought it would be and she became afraid of the birth. She had many ideas as to how the birth would be and was planning a natural childbirth; however, she backed out. She was exaggerating her pain during labor and would not cooperate with the nurse to make it easier. She was blaming her baby and her husband for her pain.*

She eventually opted for a C-section. This could have been a natural birth but the mother was acting out and there was too much drama. There was no real physical problem but nothing was working. This is the reason the doctor suggested the C-section. I am also seeing that the baby was not participating in the birth. She felt stuck and rigid and was very much afraid of coming into the world."

"During the birth, I'm sensing dullness from the baby. *He is feeling battered. This baby feels emotionally battered. When he came out of the womb, he felt extremely vulnerable. Most babies, who were in an angry or threatening womb environment, felt relief once outside the womb. However, this baby's attention was out so much during his time in the womb, and there was so much confusion and mayhem in his* *exterior environment, that he felt he was coming out into that chaotic place that he had been clairvoyantly experiencing.*

The battered feeling he is feeling now is the same feeling that he was blocking out and trying to avoid. Sometimes a person going through a bad time will distance and numb him or herself from it until it is over. Then, the person will feel 'safe enough' to feel the full brunt of the experience. That is what it is like for this baby. His attention has been out for a long time. He has been taking in what has been going on in his home situation, and now that he is in that hostile environment he is in a state of shock. He is dull and closing down."

"The father was continuing to run the show at the baby's birth. Everything had to be proper and right according to him. He was down on his wife for not being excited about having the baby. She put it on her being weary after carrying her baby for so many months."

"The baby is afraid of the sudden changes and loss of control. *He has had mental and emotional exchanges with his parents and siblings but he did not intuit that he would be on the outside with them. Right now, he is sensing that he is going to lose his life."*

This is a good example of the fact that there are many degrees of awareness a person (young or old) can have depending on the kinds of choices he or she has been willing to make.

"The mental and emotional patterns that this fetus has already put in place with reactive choices, have put him in a position of resisting and fighting the natural birth process, with which he should be cooperating. He is experiencing much confusion about what is happening. The confusion is tied to the blame he is directing at his mother. He is fixated on her and is not taking responsibility for his circumstances."

"This baby is blaming his mother for his confusion, fear, and pain. *He is also angry about the restrictions of space and movement. As this baby is being born he is angry about his circumstances and blaming his mother."*

"The baby has closed himself off from his mother's energy. She is distressed at this moment. The baby's angry and fearful thoughts and feelings are keeping him from following the intuitive knowledge now available to him. Were he to stop reacting to his mother's distress and the current physical changes and trust his inner knowledge, he would feel safe. This would help him tremendously in his birth process."

The birth is typically not an easy happening for mother or child. When we are put up against painful or difficult circumstances, it is an unusual person who embraces them without complaining—even more remarkable, for someone to be loving and caring in such situations.

As difficult as it may seem, it is important for a mother to be in a loving place during the birth. Every baby depends on his or her mother for stability, and for knowing that things are, and will be, all right. This requires a deep inner constant state of mental and emotional stability no matter what the circumstances. We see this on occasion when a person is going through something enormously painful with great courage and calm.

"I'm feeling the baby having a sense of being enclosed. It's as if the walls are closing in on him. As the contractions continue, he feels pressured and restricted. He has a sense that he can't breathe. He is feeling panicked and desperate. He is enclosed within his own emotions and is not looking out. He isn't ascertaining the reality of what is happening to him. He is rapidly going inward so he can't see that there is nothing to fear. His panic brings pain. Were he to relax and go through the process willingly, it wouldn't be such a difficult and painful happening."

Doctors sometimes say that a baby will experience contractions as a massaging of his or her body and it may feel pleasant. That is likely true in some cases. But as I have been saying throughout this book babies make psychological choices and those choices have consequences.

A baby's experience will always reflect his or her choices. Unfortunately, the medical world does not recognize this perspective. As far as I can tell, they don't include psychological choices, thoughts, and emotions into the mix, because these choices at such a young stage are not known or understood by most medical professionals. Stress and tension cause pain. When a baby is in a stressful state he or she is bound to feel the contractions as painful because the baby's mental and emotional condition is painful.

"I'm sensing almost a heartfelt cry toward his mother for help, 'Help me. Please help me.' He feels discouraged and disheartened. These feelings come from his sense of being all alone and isolated. This relates to having no real communications with his mother. He is discouraged, feeling alone and unloved. He is afraid of not getting emotional love, and, now, with this traumatic birth, he is sure that he is dying. He is reaching out for help as if he is drowning. This baby has a desperate need for emotional security and love, but he reaches in vain. After long hours of labor, intense struggle, and nervous anticipation, I'm seeing his images, 'What is going to happen to me? What will happen next?'"

A baby is like a sponge for good energy and caring attention. We have so much responsibility for creating a positive environment because a baby will always gravitate to positivity and be grateful for it.

"This baby doesn't want to be where he is. He's longing to be somewhere else. Sometimes, he is panicky

and rigid. In the next moment, he feels alone, isolated, and disheartened. Then he will flip into feeling jealous and angry. He is totally caught up in his reactive feelings that were triggered by the beginning of the contractions. I'm sensing a great lack of emotional security and a desperate desire for security from his mother."

When a baby has not had an easy time during his or her months in the womb, the birth will most definitely be a difficult one. A baby needs a lot of help and encouragement because the birth happening (the actual physical activity of it) can be traumatic. If a baby is not aware it can be a surprise and like a title wave. But when a baby has developed a trust of the mother because of her earnest caring, not only will the baby know what is happening, he or she will be sure of the mother's support and continued caring throughout the birth process.

It is not difficult to imagine how a baby about to be born could be going through much emotional trauma. During the birth, most of the time the mother's attention is on herself and her pain, or her fears. Nevertheless, much of that pain and fear did not have to be there in the first place. Many choices could have been made during the nine months, making the birth a positive happening, less fearful, and less painful.

"The baby is sensing and perceiving danger, even though there is no apparent physical danger. He's

reacting to the fearful ideas and feelings of both his parents concerning him and his birth."

In this situation, the mother had inordinate fears that the baby would have trouble getting through her "small opening." She also had other fears that were essentially unfounded. This is the reason the baby was sensing danger when there was none.

A baby in the womb picks up on any strong thought or feeling his or her mother is having. Babies look to their mothers during this time because, believe it or not, the situation is more difficult and scary for them than it is for their mothers.

"He is disoriented and incoherent because of the sudden changes in his physical surroundings. He is confused because of his unwillingness to go with the birth process. Resisting it makes him separate from this important next step in life. He is rebelling against the natural action of going towards the birth canal. He is rigid and emotionally fighting."

I think many doctors will tell you that birth, for the most part, happens automatically because it is a natural occurrence. A baby instinctively knows and obeys his or her natural inclinations. As I said before, most don't consider (because they don't know about) the acute mental and emotional abilities and experience of a baby in the womb. I don't think they believe that a baby at this stage makes psychological choices. This is a huge factor in pregnancy and birth that, as far as I know, is not being acknowledged.

"When the mother's water broke, the baby felt that he no longer had control over his movements and started panicking. He was sensing that his life was being squeezed out of him.

This fetus was afraid of the unknown, of the sudden changes, and his loss of control. Up until this time, he had been having interactions with his parents and siblings. Nonetheless, he somehow thought his life was going to be forever in the womb. The contractions came as a shock and he did not trust his experience."

"For the first time, it seems that the baby has a sense that there is a future. *In the womb, he knew he had a present and a previous experience but seemed to have no idea there was a future. This was probably because he was not looking out enough to make that connection.*

When he finally slipped through and was out in the air world, it was a relief. He received a sincere and enthusiastic welcome from the doctor and nurses, and that added to his relief. He liked the feel of his new environment and felt safe. The harsh, irritating energy that was his womb atmosphere was gone. He felt good and secure. The nurses had positive energy and he felt safe being in their presence."

"The baby is avoiding necessary signals that would help him with his birth*. I saw him asleep when the contractions started. Then, I realized that* *he was awake but hiding. He was mentally hiding while having to yield to the birth process. During his time in the womb, he had formed a definite pattern of going inward when he sensed danger. He was resisting coming out, inwardly hiding, not wanting to look out, not wanting to know what was happening. To me, he felt like someone might feel who was caught in a violent storm."*

"His mother received anesthesia, and the baby dramatically felt the effects of the drug*. His body and nervous system went numb. His energy and body functions slowed considerably. He became extremely afraid. The slowness and numbness felt like an intrinsic part of him that was new and he could not relate to it. This seemed to add to his sense of abandonment. Why? Because he had to give in to the birth process that he was unfamiliar with, and on top of that, he had to give in to the drug experience. He felt that both were being imposed upon him."*

"He felt no energetic connection or help from his mother, and received no encouragement or comfort. It was as if he was a thing not a person. His mother was asleep and feeling sorry for herself. He was in the birth canal and did not know what to expect. He was afraid of what might lie ahead."

"This was a natural childbirth and was not difficult. The birth was in a hospital without anesthesia, which was good for the baby. But, I am seeing this mother

having pain and wanting it to be over. Immediately after the birth, the mother went into feeling let down, disheartened, and that it was not worth it all. She was talking about her feelings and was told that they were normal. She was seeing the event as being over, rather than seeing the birth as a continuation or a new beginning. She expected to feel joy, but she felt disappointed, discouraged, and let down.

She is coming into some reality about the situation and realizes that she was in illusion. Now that she physically sees her baby, she is thinking that this baby girl will be the same as her boy. She will have similar frustrations and a similar ongoing battle of wills. This will probably be true because the baby is in basic opposition to her mother and in negative agreement with her father. This new baby girl is basically fearful, and her mother is basically angry."

"When the mother saw her baby, she felt relieved and happy. *Her negative feelings suddenly disappeared, and she thought to herself; how could she have felt the way she did? Her deeper feelings were still there, she was just consciously closing down on them. She did feel guilty holding her child because those feelings were still active underneath. When she breastfed him, she became irritated again, but put it onto being worn out. She gave the baby to the nurse and went to sleep."*

"The mother had a C-section. She was planning a natural childbirth but her labor was going on too long. The doctor offered her the option of a C-section. Both mother and baby were resisting the birth process. Consciously, the mother thought she was afraid because there might be something wrong with the baby. But, that was not true. Subconsciously she was afraid the baby would belong to her husband. Consciously she was afraid a girl would be no different from her three boys. This mother desperately wants her baby to love her.

She is not thinking about loving the baby. Her desperate desire to be loved by her baby is what is causing her to be panicked. She is suppressing most of this fear, although she is aware of it. The fear, especially her suppressed fear, is causing great tenseness in her body, especially in her inner organs. This is the physical reason her labor went on for so long. Her tenseness was not physically visible but her insides were extremely restricted because of her fear."

"What was the baby's experience of the C-section? I am seeing her extremely cold and tense. *She is mentally and emotionally inward. She does not want to know what is happening to her. It is as if someone has been banging her around, and she cannot move. Emotionally she has her hands over her head and face. Her eyes are closed trying to protect herself. This experience was validating the baby's mistrust of her* *mother. All at once, it was over. But, the strangeness of the birth and the welcoming hands terrified her. The baby is now under a heat lamp, but she is still rigid and afraid."*

"I see the mother feeling apprehensive now. She is surprising herself because she is rarely nervous. She is anxious about the birth, yet senses that her baby is healthy. Nevertheless, she is afraid there might be something wrong. She is telling herself that it is just her paranoia. However, the real reason for her apprehension relates to her daughter being in negative agreement with her husband. Of course, she is not consciously aware of this; and, she has built up many ideas as to what her baby will mean to her.

Subconsciously she knows her baby is fearful and has many of the patterns her husband and son have; she cannot bear the thought of that reality. The father is feeling that the situation is perfect. He has a boy and now a girl. She thinks, as usual, he is getting exactly what he wants."

Twins at birth: *"Craig is aware that something is about to happen. He is looking out and reaching out to his father; wanting his emotional help. He is apprehensive—this is about the contractions starting. Things are changing and he is alerted to that, which has brought his attention out. His attention is on his father. His brother is being born and he is about to be next.*

Craig (the fearful introverted twin) can be extremely aware when he wants to be. *It shouldn't have to take an event like this to jog him into looking outside of himself, but he is certainly looking out now. This shows that he could have put his attention out at any time if he wanted. In relation to other basically fearful fetuses, he is unusual in his present outward stance.*

Right after his birth, Dennis (the basically angry, outgoing twin) is going inward. He had control when he was in the womb and feels he has lost control. He can't move around. He feels angry and helpless. He's going inward, away from this new situation. The sense I'm getting is that he is extremely disconcerted about the new events and is traumatized by them.

Craig is also going inward after his birth but he seems to be peaceful. *To a good extent he's blocking out the new reality. It is as if he's still in the womb. He has gone back into that inner place where he is not much aware of what is going on around him. He seems to be more peaceful than his brother but still he is hiding from this new reality."*

"Even during the birth, this mother was more concerned about her physical appearance than her baby. *She had to look perfect for the doctor. She wanted the birth to be a 'thing' between her and her doctor. This is obviously a perverted pattern of behavior, but I have seen it more than once! There is play-acting* *going on. It is unfortunate that we don't just drop our hurtful patterns during an important event. It was not a difficult birth; she had anesthesia and was asleep when the baby was born. (Note: These readings were done in 1992-93, a time when anesthesia was still popular.)*

She was pretending to feel joy when seeing her baby. *Much of this was for the doctor and the people around her. She did not have any true loving feelings for her baby. The baby was at the effect of her pretense. The father was not present because he was not told in time. This had to do with the manipulation of his wife, because of her fantasies about the doctor. Her husband showed up in an angry mood; feeling that his wife ruined the situation, as she always does."*

"The mother is disappointed that she could not have a natural childbirth. Nothing went as she planned. She still believes her fears about the baby's health; even though the nurse is assuring her the baby is fine. The mother subconsciously knows she has been energetically restricting her daughter. She doesn't want the baby to connect with her husband.

She knows she feels possessive of this baby girl in ways she was not with her boys. She knows she does not want her husband to be close with their daughter. If he is better with her than she is, that will make her crazy. She knows she feels dread about the birth and feels guilty about the C-section, but does not see how that could be her fault.

Nevertheless, she cannot stop feeling guilty. Her guilt is caused by her true feelings about her daughter, and how she has already harmed her. But, she will not acknowledge this consciously. Again, if she would have the courage to verbally express the feelings she is aware of, she would be opening a door to being willing to access what she is subconsciously doing with her baby."

The mother is awake, alert, and holding her twin girls. She's amazed at how small and pretty they are. *She is relieved that the birth is over. She is riding above her feelings of wanting only one baby. She liked being taken care of in the hospital; but, once home, and alone with twins, it was back to reality and she felt dread."*

This baby is extremely un-centered. He is losing his sense of self and what to do in this moment. *Because he is caught up in images and feelings, he is sensing that something is wrong. He is feeling desperate. He perceives his situation as a confused upheaval. He is not willing to trust his inner sense. He is not at all in touch with it. He feels that something is very wrong; but this is because he wants to be in control but cannot control this happening."*

So many stories, and I have so many more. It is sad but true! Perhaps if we really started to become aware of what we do subconsciously, and, if we started to be more aware of our conscious hurtful actions (that we pretend not to be able to help or to change) maybe then, we could begin to stop some of this hurtful mental, emotional, and physical madness.

For us to do that, we would have to first believe that all this madness ***does exist*** and that ***it is*** madness. We would have to not only believe it, but we would have to know it. We would have to know it to the extent that we would want to, and be willing to, change all the hurtful intentions and potential hurtful behaviors that we harbor within ourselves.

Are we ready for such a dramatic multi-level change? Are we ready to become less selfish, rather than more? It is difficult. This is the selfish planet. It is never easy to go against selfishness. It will never happen; we will never do it unless we are willing. We need to inspire ourselves from within. We need to know and remember the good that comes with right choices.

We need to strive after that good with passionate endurance and know the contentment and joy that comes with it. Anything less, and we will not actually accomplish this goal. We will not make it. We will not experience the richness of our innate humanness. Is this planet ready for such a dramatic and positive change? Are we? I would like to think so. I know that I am not the only one.

Nine
The Saga Continues

"Every newborn baby is a true test of your character!"

Yes. A new baby is a wonderful thing! This tiny new life is an amazing addition to the family. Mom and Dad are in awe with feelings of heartfelt love and a desire to protect, care for, and nurture. No one could argue this moment—at least this conscious moment. The conscious feelings are real; to some degree they can wipe out the underneath everyday selfish concerns. Feelings of joy have the power to make all the mundane daily problems disappear.

Nonetheless, all too often for both parents it is soon back to reality. For many it is back to the everyday petty interactions as usual. Relationships are difficult because typically our self-centered concerns clash, and we must work to keep a marriage or relationship on a loving and caring plane. Adding a baby into the mix complicates and puts your selfish patterns on high red alert.

A baby can seem to require an endless stream of giving, especially at times when you just don't want to give. Or, you're half asleep and don't want to wake up. Who is going to get up? It takes an enormous amount of selfless giving to properly care for a baby, especially a newborn baby.

Every newborn baby is a true test of your character! You end up doing so many things that you didn't want to do; that you had to go against yourself to do. You had to get over yourself in so many ways.

Doing what you don't want to do, but you do it because it is the right and loving thing to do, is a true character builder. When you can do it without complaining, even to yourself, you are becoming a more loving individual with every choice you make. But, alas! So often we do not live up to our own expectations, much less anyone else's.

In this chapter, I'm going to recount some excerpts that will show you what not to do, what not to intend, how not to think, how not to feel, and how not to act. Thankfully, there are also accounts that you can use for inspiration, encouragement, and as a reminder that we can be the very best; that we can excel in our human qualities of love and loving responsibility.

When you act in these ways, you'll see that you will end up thanking your baby for what he or she has "put you through!"

A good way to understand newborns and infants is to be willing to see what they are going through emotionally and interact with them accordingly.

"This baby is about three months old. She has it relatively easy. For the most part, she can stay within herself or go outward and explore. I am seeing her exploring now. There are bright colors in her room and music playing. Her mother provides a stimulus that she can feel good about, relate to, and explore. She is continuously exploring, which is good for her sense of emotional and physical stability. If choices and situations continue the way they have been going, she will probably have minor issues with her parents, but nothing serious."

"This newborn seems to have a strong pattern of sensing that he has to control to survive. It was easier to control when he was in the womb. He could move, hide, and ignore sounds when he was threatened. Now he feels that he can't move, he has nowhere to hide, and it is difficult to avoid his siblings and mother shouting, or even making routine noises. He is not threatened by the noises themselves, but the energy inherent in the noises. The baby believes that he needs to control his environment to survive. This is a tough pattern to have to deal with in a world in which we have no real control."*

Because of our innate psychological abilities of awareness and free choice, it is literally impossible

for us to control one another essentially. When our main mode of operation is selfish it is easy to believe that we need to control to survive, or at least control to get what we want. Another point is that, attempting to control for any reason, leads to self-destruction. It diminishes our awareness of, and the experience of rightness, truth, love, and loving responsibility.

When we say that we feel out of control, that is not actually a true statement. It may feel like that is what is happening, but the opposite is in fact true. When we feel this way, we are controlling to such an extent that we are out of touch with the core of our humanness. We have become greatly out of balance, not out of control.

"At one-month old, the baby is communicating with her brother. They are exchanging images and feelings. They are in strong negative agreement with each other; this is not good. They are both basically fearful, and their mother is basically angry. The infant does reach out to her mother and at times receives warm feelings in return. Ironically, around the baby's heart center, I see feelings and ideas of love from the mother.

While at the same time, she has angry energy on the infant's head. The mother is also putting out good feelings in physical ways. This infant does not seem to be confused by this contradiction. She has been looking out for such a long time now, and has been so alert that she understands what is going on."

I believe that being an aware and smart person has much to do with choices like these that have begun in the womb.

"The baby seems to have a broad intelligence. It has to do with knowledge of feelings and experiences in a knowing way. He intimately knows the various psychological moods of both his parents. He understands a lot intuitively about the psychological world that surrounds him; he has a true sense of what is happening in his immediate environment."

Our right choices develop understanding, compassion, and many other human qualities. That is true for this baby. As young and little as he is, he is making the choices that will serve him well throughout his life.

"So far this newborn is having a hard time adjusting to her life situations. The first few months can be stressful for a newborn because of the entirely different physical circumstances. Also, when babies have the continued experience of negative energies from the mother or father, it can give a baby all kinds of frightening reactions. This mother resents having to take care of the baby when she is tired. The baby often seems to be rigid and in fear. She is physically tight but her mother does not recognize her daughter's emotional and physical conditions."

If we were to consciously understand what is going on with a newborn or an infant in the moment, I'm sure we would make choices to try to correct his or her distress. I say that because we are not monsters. Any mother (or father) with a sick child will show you that. We just need the right kinds of information. We need to know what our babies are going through psychologically.

"The baby is about two months old now. She is in good physical health. Her circulation is good. There is a lot of green energy in her third energy center, that is, her stomach area. There are also blues and all kinds of pastel colors. The baby is unusually active for her age. She is not afraid to be here, or in her physical body. This is excellent."

Even here at two months old, physical health and mental health go hand in hand. When your body feels good you are bound to feel good also. This is another area of huge misunderstanding. Most of our ailments— overweight, heart disease, etc.—are caused by psychological concerns that are suppressed, not expressed, and not dealt with; these are the subconscious triggers for wrong choices in eating and every type of dysfunction. This is a problem that we have complicated exponentially! So many seriously wrong choices, and we blame our sicknesses and pain on our age or anything but our self-destructive choices.

"This baby is now almost two months old. I'm seeing that she withdraws when her father picks her up. His energy is strong and overpowering. What he believes to be loving and endearing feelings, his baby perceives as being possessive and invasive. So, she withdraws from his emotions and physical presence. When he picks her up, he is feeling too much emotion. It is like when a person starts pinching or squeezing a baby. It is not that he pinches or squeezes her; it is more like the energy of that 'love her to death' feeling. Overpowering feelings have nothing to do with the baby and are not love."

A person, or a parent, can think he or she is feeling love for a baby but is, in fact, being hurtful emotionally and energetically. This is because the "love" is not love; it is a selfish desire. With a little introspection, the difference can become obvious.

"I am seeing the baby is energetically closing off. He is not reaching out to either parent. It is almost as if he is frozen in fear; but this may not be noticeable in a physical way. I think someone could tell that he was tense, but that would probably be the extent of it. The father is holding his baby. He is conflicted and concerned. He is thinking, 'What am I going to do with a baby? What am I going to do with a family?' He has school and so many things to think about. His attention is focused on himself, and his baby is feeling isolated."

Just because you are young and starting out in life with many aspirations and goals, it does not mean that you will not be selfish with your baby. There is so little true understanding of how we should be with a newborn. There are many fathers who think they are doing the right thing by focusing first on their ambitions and careers to the neglect of their children.

"This newborn's mother is caring about her baby's health and well-being. She wants to do everything right, which has greatly helped in her son's birth. He was relaxed and seemed to have little discomfort. He feels good to be here, warm and cozy, which translates into a sense of well-being. Because of his mother's caring and his healthy body, he is enjoying a sense of physical pleasure. There are good thoughts and feelings coming toward him from his parents. Caring and loving feelings are keeping him stable and feeling safe. This newborn is a peaceful baby and is having a good experience so far."

This baby may be a Nobel Prize winner some day!

"The baby is ten days old and is now at home. He is afraid of unfamiliar energies. His mother leaves the newborn with his grandmother. Unlike being in the hospital, this baby is finding it difficult to adjust. He is uncomfortable, uneasy, and at times afraid. There is a sense of being disgraced. His grandmother gives him affection for her own pleasure, but not in a perverse way. Nevertheless, he is feeling used.

Newborns and infants are extremely susceptible to positive and negative energies. This baby is feeling his grandmother's selfish intentions toward him. He experiences these as her using him; that is the feeling I'm getting. She believes that she has pride and joy in being the infant's grandmother. She has many ideas and illusions about him; and she is dumping an excessive amount of pseudo-positive feelings onto him. Her thoughts and feelings are not matching his experience; and they are not appropriate. He feels her tremendous lack of realness. This is confusing him and making him afraid."

When a baby is not getting direct contact he or she may feel confused and any number of feelings, including feeling disgraced. When someone is not respected as a Human Being most often the person will react with anger and indignation. My sense is that we use anger and indignation as a cover for a deeper feeling of disgrace.

An infant essentially feels and responds in all the basic ways adults do. A baby, from his or her first awakenings in the womb, has an experience of being an "*I*" and essentially will respond from that place. Babies in the womb and infants send telepathic messages long before they can talk. They have an ability to energetically and clairvoyantly see the whole picture or the actual truth of a person or situation; and they respond to that reality. Parents and grandparents may have many ideas about what it means to have a child or a grandchild. They may project their ideas about the baby onto the baby, instead of interacting in a real way.

A baby may feel confused because of the lack of realness and communication. This will also make the baby afraid, insecure, and disoriented. When parents and grandparents are stuck in their ideas about a baby, their "loving" energies go into their ideas instead of connecting with the baby.

"This baby is getting his emotional wants and needs confused with his physical needs. *His emotional needs are so strong they are eclipsing his innate natural sense, need, and desire to be fed. With his angry cry, all of his emotions about not being genuinely loved are being expressed."*

Babies possess a natural instinct to be fed and nurtured. This instinct has nothing to do with selfish desire. But when a baby is in emotional turmoil the baby may use his or her selfish desire to try to get what is wanted and will confuse emotional needs with physical needs. (Don't we all do this very thing all too often?) Anyway, when you learn to read your baby's behavior truly, you will come to know the difference.

"The baby was small. I am getting that if she had a better emotional and physical environment to grow in she would have been bigger. Being forced out of the womb seemed to be traumatic for her. There were

strange hands and strange energy capturing her. Her father was the first to hold her. His heart went out to her and he felt a connection. When he held her, the baby felt a relief and a sense of gratitude. She felt secure and her confusion began to vanish. The experience of being bombarded with energy and physical circumstances was gone, and this was a great relief. She was relaxing which was a rare experience.

In the womb, she was under almost constant pressure and stress, now she felt the absence of that and was feeling her father's caring. When the baby was given to her mother she panicked. That old feeling of hostility was back. In fear, she went inside and went to sleep as she did when she was in the womb. This mother insisted on smoking and drinking to some extent throughout her pregnancy."

Here I'd like to include some points that parents may find helpful in understanding their infants.

"When a baby has a cold, colic, or another physical ailment and feels miserable, sometimes crying uncontrollably, the physical ailment is often a trigger for a deeper emotional pain."

"When an infant becomes 'over tired' the baby will often become upset. Why is that? Why does the baby become cranky rather than peaceful and sleepy? When a baby is over tired or sick and feels miserable, he or she is most often expressing deeper emotions. The baby's defenses are down, and he or she is allowing truer feelings to surface. Also, feeling physically miserable can trigger negative emotions that are already present but not being expressed."

"All too often parents assume that the baby is emotionally upset because of a physical discomfort. Nonetheless, it is most often the other way around. When a baby feels physical discomfort he or she feels less able to handle emotional distress. Aren't we like that, too? These little examples show us that babies are just like we are only little. The more we get that reality, the more we will see, love and respect our children no matter what their age."

"Whenever a baby is being negatively emotional, it is because he or she is upset about a psychological happening. It has to do with a baby's feelings of being alone, unloved, uncared for, or generally feeling unhappy about his or her life."

"Many parents treat their infant as a baby who does not understand what is going on between his or her parents. But, as you have seen, a baby probably knows more about his or her parents than they know about each other!"

"Some parents assume that their baby has not developed enough to have mature and complex interactions and reactions. This is not true. A baby is aware of (and at the effect of) his or her parents' intentions, thoughts, feelings, and actions. The baby is aware of how his or her parents feel about each other, as well as how they feel about him or her from moment to moment."

"A baby's emotional pain is typically a reaction to his or her parents' harmful attitudes, intentions, thoughts, feelings, and actions. Perhaps this is the reason parents are slow to discover and acknowledge that the cause of their infant's emotional pain has to do with them."

"If a baby is happy most of the time and gets emotionally upset when tired or sick, the parents still have work to do."

"One good rule for parents would be to consider or assume that their baby's emotional unhappiness has essentially little to do with his or her physical discomfort."

"A baby can be uncomfortable or sick without being irritable. Irritability is an emotional state that has to do with psychological reasons, not physical ones."

"A baby's cry or emotional expression can tell a parent exactly what is going on emotionally. A baby's emotional misery becomes obvious when he or she is sick or tired. These are good times to tune-in to the baby's real reasons for his or her emotions, rather than dismiss them by putting them onto a physical cause."

"A baby has a wide range of emotions that parents can see, when they are willing to acknowledge that their negativity or neglect (even in small ways) may be the trigger for their baby's emotional discomfort."

"Parents would have to be willing to be wrong about their ideas about their infants and themselves. Parents would have to be willing to see that, when their infants are in emotional pain, it is because their babies are reacting to their wrong choices. This means they would have to be willing to be wrong about many things that they, so far, have not been willing to be wrong about."

"It is much easier for infants to be happy and content when they have parents who are willing to be truthful with themselves and each other."

"When parents are willing to look at themselves in truth and change the negatives that need to be changed, their baby will have a happier emotional life."

If these facts seem complicated, unreal, disconcerting, impossible, couldn't be true, too difficult, way beyond me, crazy, no way to know what is going on here; if you are saying, *"Does what I do really affect my baby that much? I am too worried already; this would just make me worse. I don't know how to do this even if I wanted to. If I do try it, how will I know I am succeeding? Who is going to tell me if I'm doing it wrong? Won't my imagination run away with me one way or another? How do I tell what is real and what I'm making up? I could be making myself a monster or a saint or anything in-between."*

You will not have an answer for any of your concerns unless you try. You will probably go through all or most of the thoughts and feelings I've just described. However, if you work consistently, and if you persevere because you want to understand your baby, you will ultimately succeed. That may happen without you even realizing it; when we are working to be aware and loving, we often don't recognize our success because we are focusing on what has yet to be done.

Having said that, when you strive to have genuinely caring intentions toward your baby, you will find ways to do all the things I've described. You will accomplish your goal. Your baby will love you in return, and those expressions and feelings will certainly be well worth the effort.

Ten
The Process of Essential Change

---

*"For a choice to be truly right, it must also
be true, loving, and lovingly responsible."*

**Before we can commit to changing on an essential
level it is necessary to recognize the most basic
reason we suffer as humans.** It is important to see
that our choices are the reasons we suffer mentally,
emotionally and physically.

It seems to me that Human Beings were created
with a very definite purpose. We don't get to choose
our purpose. It has been chosen for us. I say that
because when we don't fulfill that purpose we suffer.
Not fulfilling that purpose is the cause of all our pain
in its various forms. Our pain is the effect of choices
to go against our innate purpose. That choice is what
creates all the chaos, the confusion about how we are,
and our pain in all its forms.

*I believe that our purpose as Human Beings is
to express love to all the life around us, period. No
excuses. No arguments.*

Why do I believe that? I endeavor to view life as a psychological scientist. Get to the truth inside and out. To me, it appears that all of our suffering is, and has been, created by choices to oppose love in all the many resourceful ways we choose to do that.

We were created with a very clear compass. When we use that compass wonderful, magical things happen within and without us. But, we only view those things as wonderful and magical because we use our innate compass so infrequently! If we used that compass every time we made a choice, truly wonderful and magical would be the norm, and our lives would be as we cannot yet imagine.

When we are not aligned with our purpose to love all the life around us, we suffer. As I have said throughout this book, we have complicated ourselves so greatly with our wrong choices that, for the most part, it is difficult to know just where to begin.

Essential change needs to be a life's work. No matter where we find ourselves on the continuum of selfishness and wrong choices, we all have work to do. I'm not just talking about changing obvious behaviors such as indulging in an overwhelming desire for alcohol, sex, drugs, food, or any other destructive activity that we like to call "addictions." It is all the seemingly little things that keep us from experiencing a true sense of self and well-being.

When we do something that we know is wrong or we give-in to an "addiction" we often say we are only human. So, we end up doing that same thing again and again. But, as I said before, the phrase "only human" is a huge misrepresentation of how we were created and who we were truly meant to be. I think it is one of our most basic and widespread rationalizations for not doing what we know we can do and should do.

We all need to work exactly where we are; we need to work on the biggest and smallest disruptions within our psyches.

If we have so-called major addictions, that is where we need to work; if we get angry a lot and say mean things, that is our challenge. If we are afraid to be honest with a spouse or partner, we need to start identifying the patterns that are under our fear. No matter what the behavior, we need to stop ourselves (right then) and strive to understand the "whys" of our thoughts, feelings, and actions. If we do this every time (or even almost every time) we will change ourselves dramatically.

Starting in the womb, our wrong choices were, and always are, reactions. Even our first agreements with our parents when we were still fetuses were reactions. We agreed out of fear, or to get a benefit that we felt we needed. Just look at the fetus that chooses to withdraw to an extreme. Those choices, which result in extreme inwardness in the womb, cause all kinds of interactive problems for the child growing up and on through adulthood.

Much of what we consider to be a normal part of life, genetic, or an accident, I believe is a consequence of wrong choices, choices that began in the womb. I know this may sound implausible. However, from what I see, we humans are in so much trouble psychologically and have no true solution. Medical professionals admit that they only treat the symptoms and do not have a cure. There has to be a better way! I think we are very far-a-field from the truth about many of our behaviors that are now deemed to be genetic, or in some way a physical mishap with the cause somewhere outside of ourselves.

It seems unreasonable to be required to have so much (total) responsibility for our choices and our conditions, which are the results of our choices. But, as unreasonable and unfair as that may seem, it is what _**is**_, and we feel the effects of our choices (positive or negative) at every moment of our lives.

Let's talk about reactions. We usually think we are reacting only when it is an obvious reaction to a person or a situation. They act and we react. That is not really the way it works. Everything you do is a reaction when you are choosing to be selfish; in some way choosing wrongly.

Why is this so? I'm not totally clear on this; however, I know that our very first choice was somehow a decision to approach life, and life's situations, from either an angry or a fearful stance. That choice put us in opposition to love, or having a loving position. This happened so early that it is difficult to see how, or why, we might have chosen that way. But, if we had not chosen that way, we would be in an essentially loving position and stance. A loving attitude would be our base of operation, not anger or fear.

Our conflict starts early because we are basically in opposition to love. Instead of approaching life situations from a place of love, we have chosen anger or fear. We must work against that choice, for anger or fear, to be loving Human Beings. Don't you ever wonder why it is often difficult to care, and truly love without thinking of yourself? Well, I believe that this is the reason. It is because so early on we have chosen to be in opposition to love. We have chosen either anger or fear to be our mode of operation, not love.

Let's look at some of our more obvious reactions. First let me say, when you react it is *your* reaction, end of story. It is not "*You made me react.*" Or "*I would have never done that if it weren't for you,*" etc., etc. We are so often entrenched in this kind of thinking. Most of us blame our parents for how we turned out, especially if we didn't "*turn out*" the way we wanted, or they wanted.

Look at where you are, and you will know that this is where you wanted to be. Your choices determine

how you "turn out."

Having read the womb baby excerpts it should be clear that, although your parents are not directly responsible for how you have chosen, they hold much responsibility for how they treated you. To the extent that they have been the trigger for your reactions, they are responsible, not for your choices to react, but for their choices concerning you.

Our reactions are <u>our</u> reactions. Unless we hold firm to this truth and understand it we will not have the willingness to change. We must be in a position of being willing rather than willful, to change in right and loving ways. Blame is like a dark shadow over the truth; you can sort of see the truth but you don't get to see the entire truth. Anything less than the entire truth is a lie; you can do nothing good with a lie. When you blame yourself, it is the same story; just see the truth about yourself and change it. Anything more is drama!

We sometimes feel that we are acting without purpose, but that is never true. We always have a purpose for everything we think, feel, and do. That purpose is our motive; it is our intention.

Every choice counts. This may sound and feel overwhelming, but when you observe yourself in every moment, you will see that from moment to moment you are choosing. Subconsciously you already know every choice you made and why you made it. If you want to become less complicated and less stressful, make your intentions and choices conscious.

When you choose to notice your choices, you will become consciously aware of them. If you practice this for a while, it will become like an automatic part of your conscious awareness. You will become infinitely more responsible for your intentions, choices, and behaviors in general. The less routine you can make your thoughts; the less reactive you will become. Observing repeated mindless thoughts, and changing them as they come up, is also a good exercise to help you get a clear perspective. Besides, it will help practically. because it will bring your focus back to what you should be thinking and doing.

Our pretend reality has probably been an epidemic since the beginning of time! We all pretend to some degree. That is why we take it as normal and continue on in our stressful, painful, and less-than-satisfying lives. We live painful lives often without even realizing how disconnected and badly we feel. Think about your behavior. How much of it is troubled, anxious, angry, fearful, or stressed in relation to your everyday life? Facing yourself and understanding why you do something may seem difficult. But, thinking about doing it and, in fact, doing it are two entirely different realities. When you do it, it not only becomes easy but it will be interesting. You will become a scientist in your own life. Besides that, understanding will weaken your desires to react instead of act!

Working to change what we know is wrong within ourselves is a path that will make us feel better, not worse. It is a way to become more genuine. It is a way for us to be who we are—that is, our character will be our personality. No division. No pretense, what a relief!

Essential change is complicated because it is not only your wrong choices that create your living experience; it is the wrong choices of others. Wrong choices impact everyone. Some are global but most are close to home. When you react to a wrong choice with a wrong choice, you become involved and escalate the situation. You will feel the negative effects exponentially. This is true because in that process, you will activate many of your own patterns that match the other person's patterns. Then the interaction escalates. However, if you choose to act "out of the box" you will be able to see the interaction, the other person, or situation clearly. You will have a right perspective in which to act; you won't be caught up in the play of feelings, ideas, and opinions.

An important part of this process is to change the way you think. Change your perspective to value and observe what is true rather than what you think is true. Look consistently for what is true. There are many realities that are horrifyingly negative and hurtful. Facing the truth of these kinds of realities is sometimes necessary and can be extremely painful. Also, we all have negative and painful experiences recorded within us that we should not ignore because they are a part of the truth about us.

There are those who proclaim that everything is positive, that it is a learning experience, or happens for some good reason. That kind of thinking is completely wrong. Not only is it wrong, but those ideas can envelop a person in an illusionary, hurtful bubble. That bubble can lead a person down a progressing avenue of unreality, while making seriously wrong choices every step of the way.

There are many arguments about truth, but we all know that truth does exist. When we get our excuses and opinions out of the way, the truth is not so difficult to see. When you consistently change your wrong intentions and choices that you are consciously aware of, you will begin to perceive, understand, and change your wrong subconscious intentions and choices. Understanding your patterns of behavior will help you in this endeavor.

Professionals confuse us and misguide us about behavior patterns; first by calling them *"Defense Mechanisms"* (invented by Freud). Our negative behavior patterns are supposed to be a defense against ourselves? Does that even make sense?! Secondly, they confuse us by saying that our behavior patterns appear to be a part of our very nature. They may be our "norm" but they are never our nature. The newest theory is that our behavior patterns when they are extreme (mental illnesses) are brain diseases. Mental illness is such an involved condition, and there is so much to be explained. However, because of my forty-year career of reading countless subjects, with all kinds of mental illnesses, I would have to stand firm in my conviction that we create our mental and emotional experiences whatever they may be.

I believe that professionals have put the "cart before the horse." What they find in the brain that they claim causes disease, such as Alzheimer's, has been imprinted there by many, many avoidant (and other) wrong choices of the patient over the course of a life-time. When we make seriously wrong choices (choices that we most often hide and excuse for one reason or another) over a lifetime, we become incredibly complicated!

Without the right information, there is no way to get out of the maze. We have that information right within us. We don't have to go far to know how to get out of the maze of our behavior patterns.

We need to trust our inner sense of what is right and act on it. That is a totally other kind of experience than acting on our ideas of what we think is right and good. When we practice consulting our inner sense of right, we may not get it right the first few times, or even the first twenty, thirty, or fifty times. Nevertheless, we will know that we *didn't* get it right and *that* is a huge step in the right direction. Then we will try again. This takes courage to be different, but most of all it takes a willingness to do what is essentially right according to your own inner compass.

More about our patterns of behavior: We need to de-program. We need to de-energize our patterns by understanding and minimizing our programmed responses. That choice may sometimes seem impossible because the idea of doing that will hit the core of our selfishness. But, when we do it, there is relief, and we see that it was not as impossible as we had imagined. Each choice against selfishness makes the next choice easier. I must note another aspect of this dynamic. As you go deeper into the elimination of selfish choices, you will come up against more core level patterns, and this makes it a never-ending challenge.

Patterns have been built by many choices to enact them over the years of your life. The stronger the pattern, the more you need to act to defuse it. The less energy in our patterns the easier it is to go against them, and the easier our lives become.

When you are following your inner sense of what is right in a situation, your ideas are not in control. You don't know how you will be until the circumstance of the next moment presents itself. The more right choices you make, the more you will understand this reality and the less complicated you will become. When we act in this way enough times, a pattern will lose its power over us. Choice by choice we will be de-energizing our patterns and all of their related ideas and feelings.

We need to do this every time the urge to enact a pattern comes up. Consistency is important, but two steps forward and one step back may be our progress, until we really *want* to change enough to be *willing* to change. Taking these steps will bring you to a place of reality and give you a perspective that may be totally new. I think you will find that it is a way of life and living that is absolutely worth the consistent and sustained determination.

Conclusion

If you have read through this book to get to this page, Congratulations and Thank You!

If my words resonate with you, and you want to begin (or continue; I know I'm not alone in striving to live this way) this journey to combat your selfishness at its core, I commend you!

If you are just beginning to consciously recognize, identify, acknowledge, and act against your core selfish intentions, thoughts, feelings, and actions, you will be in for quite a ride. As much as you think you want to do this, when *"push comes to shove"*, watch out! You will not!

You will wiggle this way and that way. You will make elaborate excuses and believe them. You will feel like a two-year-old stamping your feet and saying, *"Why do I have to be the one who is wrong all the time? Why can't I have what I want? This is too hard. I just can't. I'm embarrassed. How can I say I'm wrong when I desperately want to be right?"*

Anger and tantrums will erupt, and when the dust settles you will have either made the right choice or not, but you will know the truth, and consciously experience the effects of your choice. You will not be able to escape that truth and that is a great benefit. If you made the wrong choice you will feel bad, but with a desire to make the right choice the next time a situation arises.

There will be times when you are afraid, even terrified to tell the truth when it is appropriate, necessary, or plainly the right thing to do. You are sure you will lose, and maybe you will. You will first feel that it is totally impossible. You just can't. It is so far beyond you that you make up reasons why it is really not necessary. It is not the end of the world. It is not so important. If you let it go for a few days, it won't matter anymore; it will just fade away.

Nonetheless, you have made a wrong choice. Are you going to make the right choice now, or wait until the next time? If you do it now, the next time will be easier. If you wait until the next time, you will probably make the same wrong choice again.

These are two basic examples of opportunities where you can meet the core of your selfishness and slay it. When you do this consistently, even if you don't make the right choice the first few times, eventually you will. Then, with each time you face that fear, terror, or angry tantrum, you will have increased your willingness to do what you know is the right thing to do in the next situation that presents itself.

When you work consistently, in time the tantrums and terror will subside. You will begin to see that this is the way you should be; your awareness of what is right, and your choices for that right, will become an everyday, almost automatic choice. It will be your first inclination to make that right choice. You will occasionally get stuck in your patterns of selfishness and you won't want to make the right choice, but you will move on from this place.

When your selfishness scale tips, and your selfish mode is 10 percent and your willing mode is 90 percent, you will experience your life (and yourself) in a totally new way. You will look for the right choice and do it. You will look for the right way to go and take it. It doesn't mean that you won't make selfish choices, (that darn 10 percent) but when you realize it, you will stop, change, and do better the next time.

Your focus will not be on what you may want for yourself, or even for others; you won't be thinking of yourself first, or even at all. The topic of you just never comes up. Having said that, your life will have worries, desires, some heartbreak, the pain of another's suffering at home, or across the globe, and the stress of dealing with your everyday life.

But—and this is a huge but—you will experience an inner contentment, an excitement when you see genuinely good things happen, momentary joy at little discoveries within yourself and the life around you. In effect, you will approach yourself, and all the life around you, in an entirely new way. It will be a loving way that takes no effort and produces much contentment and joy.

Are we ready for such an adventure? Well, then, let's get started!